Blossoms by the Sea

MAKING RIBBON FLOWERS FOR QUILTS

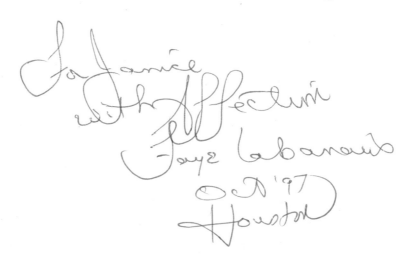

Blossoms by the Sea

MAKING RIBBON FLOWERS FOR QUILTS

by Faye Labanaris

Foreword by Elly Sienkiewicz

American Quilter's Society

P. O. Box 3290 • Paducah, KY 42002-3290

Located in Paducah, Kentucky, the American Quilter's Society (AQS), is dedicated to promoting the accomplishments of today's quilters. Through its publications and events, AQS strives to honor today's quiltmakers and their work – and inspire future creativity and innovation in quiltmaking.

Library of Congress Cataloging-in-Publication Data

Labanaris, Faye.
      Blossoms by the sea : making wired-ribbon flowers for quilts / by Faye Labanaris ; foreword by Elly Sienkiewicz.
        p. cm.
      Includes bibliographical references.
      ISBN 0-89145-862-X
      1. Appliqué--Patterns. 2. Patchworks. 3. Album quilts--United States. 4. Flowers in art. 5. Thaxter, Celia 1835–1894.
I. Title.
TT779.L25   1996   95-48093
746.44'5–dc20   CIP

Additional copies of this book may be ordered from: American Quilter's Society, P.O. Box 3290, Paducah, KY 42002-3290 @ $24.95. Add $2.00 for postage & handling.

Copyright: 1995, Faye Labanaris

Printed by IMAGE GRAPHICS, INC., Paducah, Kentucky

Dedication

*This book is dedicated to
three very special people in my life.*

Thank you to

*My friend, Bonnie B. Quimby
for first acquainting me with Celia and her garden*

*My teacher, Elly Sienkiewicz,
for introducing me to Baltimore Album Quilts*

*My mother, Orania Lappas Samaras,
for teaching me to sew*

*Without these three people, this book and quilt
would not have happened.*

Acknowledgments

A person can make a quilt by themselves, but a book is a different story. It takes many to insure its completion. As a first time author, I am realizing just how much a group effort it is to produce a book. I truly could not have done this first book by myself. To all those involved in the many stages of this book's production, I thank you for such a wonderful job!

I would like to thank:

The American Quilter's Society and its publisher Meredith Schroeder, for taking a chance with such an unusual book.

Victoria Faoro, for her superb editorial skills and patience, above and beyond, in dealing with all the concerns of a new author. Her calmness, professionalism, and insight into my first book gave me much encouragement in times of doubt.

Mary Lou Schwinn and Marty Bowne for their suggestion that I write a book about Celia's quilt.

Elly Sienkiewicz, my teacher and my friend, for her Foreword to the book and her continued excitement and support from the first moments of this book.

Elizabeth Akana, my friend full of the Aloha spirit, who also shared in the book's first moments and continued to give me support throughout.

Bonnie B. Quimby, for assuring me that I could do this. She never doubted my completion or success for a moment. Her faith and friendship will always be with me, especially now that she is with Celia.

Star Island Corporation and Vaughn Cottage/Thaxter Museum curators Kristen Start and Sarah Giffen and others associated with Star Island; Ed Rutledge and Donna M. Titus for their contribution of material; Jane Vallier, author of *Poet on Demand*, for encouraging me to tell Celia's story through flowers; Peter Randall, publisher of Shoals related materials and photographer; Fred McGill resident historian on Star Island, who personally knew Oscar Laighton and shared many stories with me; Sandy Smith, collector of Celia's books, for her gift of *A Heavenly Guest* when I so urgently needed it and for giving me the pleasure of touching some of Celia's china.

Special Collections librarians at Portsmouth Library, Portsmouth, NH; Miller Library, Colby College, Maine; Shoals Marine Lab, Cornell University, Ithaca, NY; UNH Photography Department, Shoals Collections, Durham, NH.

Tina Gravatt and Nancy Emerson for early draft reading and encouragement. Fellow needleworkers Linda Hilliard, Ellen Peters, JoAnne Joy for proofing flower instructions. My sister, Joanna Samaras, for her title suggestions which started a whole chain reaction of title suggestions. Eugenia Barnes, for her appraising skills and her sensitivity into the quilt's spirit and its effect on people.

My family for allowing me to do what makes me happy and especially to my first born son, Andrew, for his drawings; to number two son Tom for his critique and quilt understanding; and to my husband Nick, without whose care of the family and technical computer skills, this book would not have been possible!

Old friends and new, my students who are the Good Ladies of Baltimore North, guild members, people who have heard my lecture or seen the quilt, thank you for your excitement, for your desire to hear more of Celia's story. This book is for you.

Faye Labanaris
December 1995

Contents

Foreword

Several summers ago, outside an Album Quilt Class at the Vermont Quilt Festival, I met Faye Labanaris: A pretty, strong-minded woman with a spiritedness in her Mediterranean-dark eyes that caught my attention. In those years, Faye, a born teacher, was piloting an experimental science program for her local school district, while teaching quiltmaking on a regional scale and making prize-winning quilts. She did all this within the arms and obligations of a marriage blessed by a most supportive husband and two thriving sons. I didn't realize then that I would come to know Faye well.

In time, I would also learn that when Faye pronounces that you need to see something, you listen. A plain-spoken woman, she has perfected the art of verbal simplicity. I loved the three-line endorsement she gave on the back of my *Design a Baltimore Album Quilt* book. "Most necessary!" ran her entire first sentence. Now, here is Faye, telling us that there are quite wondrous things to be learned from a largely forgotten nineteenth-century poet, Celia Laighton Thaxter.

The audience to whom Faye initially addressed Celia's awakening are quiltmakers. Like a quiltmaker's threaded legacy, Celia's poetry and prose left a tangible testament that speaks to us still. Through her written work, we can share her lyrical vision and the intimate kinship she felt with the corner of the world where she had been planted. Celia's expressive art may reveal something new about ourselves. Her Victorian life delivers a message for our modern times.

As a quiltmaker I love the Album style, as much for its stitched traces of a time gone by as for its reflection of the feelings of women who have gone before me. Just as Celia's eloquent written words reflect a passionate life of the mind, the Album quilters' needlework legacies revealed their lives, concerns, values, and dreams. By viewing this work, I feel rooted as part of an ancient continuum, helping me to understand where I've come from and where my daughter, Katya's, world will be going. I can see more clearly how virtuous values thrive when cherished, how fundamental mores have been preserved, and how a focused pursuit of beauty in everyday life can increase the moral wealth of man.

It intrigues me that Celia Thaxter created her art and won her fame along a path ever impeded by obstacles. Such a difficult life makes her an even more inspiring exemplar for us today. Life is never easy. Yet Celia chose, above all, to extol the beauty in her day-to-day existence and, by so doing, lived a life well worth examining.

Celia was known for her dauntless industry and compelling presence. Faye possesses these traits as well. Both exemplify a connection between a love of the flowering earth and a life of the mind that makes sense. During the past dozen years, Album quiltmakers have grown in vast numbers, in skillful self-expression, and in fellowship. Many have come to consider themselves and their fellow quiltmaker comrades on a peaceful foray into the past that involves both a voyage into times "just beyond memory" and an inward journey. Celia's relentless vigor and passion for beauty both echo this odyssey on which so many Album quiltmakers find themselves.

At first, Album quiltmaking drew us inward. Specifically, we gravitated toward the Baltimore-style appliqué, the likes of which we'd never known before. We wondered, could we modern mortals even dream to paint so finely with cloth? We learned that not only could we duplicate these efforts, but, on occasion, surpass them. Then, we looked deeper into the antique Album framework. We learned the antebellum Baltimore Albums offered up a wealth of decorative imagery – a collection of classic patterns. At first, we faithfully reproduced these traditions, an act which taught the style so well that it began to bloom anew. We undertook magical manipulations of cloth that gave a third dimension to our flowers. Further, we came to understand how these very blossoms could convey a wealth of hidden sentiment. Then, in a whirl of ribbons and trims, calicoes and cut cloth, we were off down the garden path creating our own magic. In this book, you will see that when Faye stitched her Album quilt tribute to the poet Celia, she paid homage with arms full of artful flowers.

But, there was more to those old Album quilts than the appealing place-ment of cloth upon cloth. Those quilts convey an intensity and a spirituality that, once it catches your interest, will be as compelling to you as it was to me. In my first book, *Spoken without a Word*, I tried to translate Album quilts' extensive use of symbolism and reveal how these quilts functioned as windows into the souls of the women who made them. This symbolic use of images reveals how quiltmakers present the world around them in the hope of understanding the world in which they live. Faye's Celia Thaxter quilt reflects a fervor for botany and blooms, a devotion to her own coastal New Hampshire, a connection with the sisterhood of women, a sustaining faith, and a love of both virtue and natural beauty as expressed in poetry and quiltmaking.

How natural, then, that we who come to quiltmaking with open hearts and minds anticipate hearing what Faye Labanaris can tell us about a kin-dred creative spirit: Celia Laighton Thaxter. Celia's message from the last century can help us ready ourselves to meet the future. What better protec-tor, against the unknown, than the accumulated wisdom, the gathered blos-soms, the virtuousness of this fine woman from the past? So, enter now the poetess Celia, with all thanks to the quiltmaker, Faye.

Elly Sienkiewicz
Washington, D.C. April 1995

A TRIBUTE TO CELIA THAXTER (1835 – 1894), 70" X 70", 1994. Faye Samaras Labanaris.

Introduction

I hadn't planned on writing a book. My tribute to Celia Thaxter was to be just a quilt, a quilt that told the story. But I was urged by many who saw my quilt to tell the story behind the quilt, to tell of Celia Thaxter's life and garden and the peace and beauty of nature that I felt through Celia's own words and her flowers.

This book is the story of that quilt, why it was made, how it was made, and for whom it was made. The quilt tells the story of Celia Thaxter's life, (1835 – 1894) and her treasured island garden. Although Celia lived over 100 years ago, her legend and lore have not died. Her thoughts, her words, her poetry, and her garden still live on.

I have tried to capture the essence of Celia in a quilt that depicts her life and her garden, and to share her again with the world through her words and flowers. Techniques and patterns for many of the flowers in the quilt will enable the readers who quilt to re-create these with their own hands. Also included are Celia's poetry, prose, garden wisdom, and her life as made known to us through the many letters she wrote to her family and friends.

The actual making of this quilt is also quite a story. I kept a sketch book/journal of its progress from its conception to its completion. Many strange events contributed to the making of this quilt. It's almost as if Celia herself were helping.

The retelling of Celia's story in the form of a quilt was influenced by three events in my life. The first was the gift of *An Island Garden* written by Celia Thaxter. This birthday present from a very special friend in the early 1980's was the perfect gift for gardening inspiration and 10 years later, for Celia's quilt.

The second event occurred in August 1992. I was spending my first week on the Isles of Shoals, Star Island, as part of a conference, LIFE ON A STAR I, sponsored by the Unitarian/Universal Church and I was teaching CELIA'S BOUQUET as a five day quilting class to the conferees. This miniature appliquéd wallhanging of dimensional blooms was inspired by Celia's *An Island Garden* book. I had been assigned a sleeping room under the eaves on the third floor of cottage A. I soon found out that this was Celia's brother Oscar Laighton's room during his retirement years on Star Island.

Oscar was the last old man of the Isles of Shoals and lived to be ninety-nine years and nine months old. Since I was sleeping in his room, I became very interested in finding out more about Celia's brother. I purchased his book *Ninety Years on the Isles of Shoals* at the island book shop and read it as soon as I arrived home.

Near the end of the book, I read the brief paragraph Oscar devoted to

Celia's death. One sentence jumped out at me and touched my heart: "As I saw Celia lying there, the thought came to me that surely anyone so gifted and beloved could not be lost forever."[1]

I answered (to myself...and to Oscar) that she is not lost! Celia's spirit has never really died in the seacoast area of New Hampshire and southern Maine. Through her books, her poetry, her painted china, her garden, she is still here.

The third event occurred several months later when C&T Publishing Company announced their Baltimore Album Revival Contest in the fall of 1992. This contest was based on the series of books, *Baltimore Beauties and Beyond*, written by Elly Sienkiewicz. There would be three categories in this contest. The first was "Revival of a Classic Style"; the second, "Beautifully Innovative"; and the third "Reflective of Particular Lives and Times." I knew as soon as I read the third category that I would enter the contest and make my Baltimore Album quilt as a tribute to Celia Thaxter.

Many strange events and unusual coincidences occurred while I was making this quilt. For example, I started sewing the blocks on the first day of spring, March 21, and finished the completed top on Celia's birthday, June 29. I hadn't planned this coincidence; it was just the way it happened.

At times it was almost as if Celia herself were helping me. Whenever I was unsure as to my next step in the quilt's construction, I would relax and reread Celia's *An Island Garden* book or look at photographs in *Childe Hassam: An Island Garden Revisited,* by David Curry Park. Before too long a solution to the problem would present itself and I would then execute it in cloth.

August 26, 1994, was the 100th anniversary of Celia's death. By my making this quilt and retelling her story in various classes and lectures across the country, her story is again being told. She had a gift with words. Many of the explanations and descriptions in the book are Celia's own because her words are so eloquent. Only two of her books are available today, *An Island Garden* and *Among the Isles of Shoals* (reissued on the 100th anniversary of her death, 1994).

Celia's words and flowers gave many moments of joy and comfort to her family and friends over one hundred years ago. Through the quilt and this book, I hope her words and flowers will continue to give comfort and inspiration for the next hundred years.

In my journal I recorded inspirations for blocks – and the possibilities, problems, questions that my reading and thinking brought to mind. My journal became my project confidant. Slowly the design for A TRIBUTE TO CELIA THAXTER (1835 – 1894) emerged.

Journal Notes — The Beginning

January 1, 1993... Intense border of Celia's flowers! Sky blue background, five-block set on point.

I had recently finished a commission quilt and liked its set of five blocks on point. This set became my starting point for the design of my quilt. I would surround the blocks with a border of Baltimore flowers. As I got into the actual design process, I became intrigued with a photograph and painting which viewed Celia's garden through an arch of flowers. I tried to incorporate that arch design into the border .

I spent every free moment I had reading and rereading Celia's *An Island Garden* book and other books about her life and island for inspiration. Inspirations for blocks came fast and furious. I kept a journal beginning on January 1, 1993, of these inspirations (quotes, descriptions, etc.) for potential block designs.

Soon I had enough potential blocks for three quilts, but had to limit myself to one quilt's worth, for the moment. At first I thought about setting the blocks with a sashing of vines between the blocks. This changed to simply blocks without sashing, because I wanted the blocks to stay as a unified area. The five blocks on point needed filler blocks to square off the set. Quarter corner blocks and half blocks were incorporated into the design. I now had thirteen possible sites to tell Celia's story.

January 26, 1993... have come up with a basic plan. The border will be the most dynamic part of the quilt. Besides being filled with flowers, it will have banners of poetry and cameos of people, etc... Filler triangles?... Separate border with fence detail?... Width?

How to Make Wire-edged Ribbon Flowers

Wire-edged ribbon was first manufactured during the nineteenth century in the Southern Lyon/Midi region of France. Rather than being a quilter's tool, it was used in French confectionery shops to wrap their presentations of sweets. It is still used today.

Originally made of silk, today's wire-edged ribbon is made from rayon and is entirely colorfast. In addition to manufacturers in France, factories in Germany, Switzerland, and the United States now make a wide range of colors in both solid and variegated shades. These ribbons are as much a feast for the eyes as the delicious French confections were for the palate.

Today's high quality wire-edged ribbon has a thin copper wire along the selvage edge so it will not rust. Beware, however, of inexpensive wire-edged craft ribbon not constructed with copper wire. Less expensive metal may rust. Double check by pulling back a tiny portion of the fabric covering the wire in the selvage edge.

Wire-edged ribbon comes in many colors, textures, weights, and widths. The most popular widths are #3 (¾"), #5 (1"), and #9 (1½"). These particular widths will make almost any dimensional structure which can be appliquéd to a background. For example, you can make a beautiful Baltimore Blue Bow for an appliquéd floral block by tying the actual ribbon into a bow, flattening and molding it for appliqué purposes. The ribbon can also be used for appliquéd woven baskets. If the ribbon is too wide, simply fold to the desired size. Once the shape is constructed, simply tack the ribbon in place with matching thread.

Flowers can be made realistic or impressionistic. Each individual flower reflects the maker. It is impossible to fail. It is also very simple and more economical than you would expect. Many flowers can be made with less than 12 inches of ribbon. You can use unwired ribbon to fashion certain types of flowers and leaves, but a different effect will be achieved. Every scrap of wire-edged ribbon can be used. For example, use tiny scraps to stuff ribbon berries or save the excess wire trimmed from a gathered rose to quickly make ribbon leaves.

There are a few basic rules and sewing tips when working with wire-edged ribbon. For sewing ribbon flowers, I recommend the use of milliners' needles. These 1½" long needles are thin and slide easily through the wire-edged ribbon. Use paper scissors, rather than good fabric scissors, for cutting wire-edged ribbon.

When sewing these flowers, I use a double strand of matching thread for strength because much of the flower's construction involves gathering and pulling. With this method, be sure to pull the gathers every few inches. This gather-as-you-sew process will prevent the thread from twisting and breaking.

When the wire itself is used to gather the ribbon, simply hold the wire and gently slide the ribbon along the wired edge toward the middle section of the ribbon's length. Do not rush or pull or the wire may break and you'll have to resort to needle and thread. Reverse the ribbon and gather the other end in the same manner.

Do not drop your cut ends of snipped wire onto the floor. They are dangerous to vacuum cleaners and pets. Never use your teeth to hold the wire while you gather/slide the ribbon. You may crack the enamel on your teeth.

Wire-edged ribbon flowers almost make themselves. Whenever I teach this technique, the "first-time rose makers" cannot wait for the introductory directions to finish before they begin to make their first rose. Instructions for over one dozen wire-edged flowers from Celia's garden will enable you to create a bouquet of lasting beauty with your own hands.

Block One:

Celia's Profile

Celia Thaxter: Poet, Gardener, Lover of Nature

*"The air was sweet with flowers that day,
mingled with the pungency of the sea,
when a daughter, to be named Celia,
was born to Eliza & Thomas Laighton"* [1]

Rosamond Thaxter
Sandpiper

Featured Flower:

Celia's Sculptured

Rose, Instructions

p. 23

Celia's birth on June 29, 1835, in Portsmouth, New Hampshire, was an occasion of great joy for her parents, who had lost an infant daughter less than a year earlier. Little did these joyous parents know that this second daughter, who at a very early age began writing stories and verses, would go on to write over 300 poems in her lifetime. One of America's first women authors, by the late nineteenth century she was probably its best known female poet and naturalistic writer. Her last book, *An Island Garden,* was published just before her death in 1894, and is still widely read as a gardening literature classic.

This last book served as my introduction to Celia Thaxter. With loving descriptions of her flowers, Celia very graciously welcomed me into her garden and into her life.

Sandpiper, a biography written by Celia's granddaughter Rosamond Thaxter, provides an intimate and authentic account of the burdens and responsibilities she faced as a daughter, wife, mother, and artist. Similarly,

it offers an intimate look at the moments of peace and beauty she found in her gardening and her flowers. Celia especially loved roses! She grew them, and she wrote about them. Traveling in 1880 with her brother Oscar, she wrote to her son from Florence, Italy: "O John, John, the roses! The hill side at San Miniato is pink and crimson with them, all sorts of flowers in full blaze....The roses in this town! I shall never forget them – the streets seem to bloom – every other person carries them – they are sold at every corner, a peck for 3 cents....My lap is full of roses." [3]

Celia loved to *wear* roses, too. Her garments were always black, white, or gray, but to them she would pin a beautiful flower, more often than not, a rose. She comments in a February 25, 1861 letter to her mother: "I wore the meek-colored silk gown, Mother dear, with the light blue trimming, plain lace sleeves, no bows or ribbons....I had a lovely spray of white roses, half opened buds, and one salmon colored rose, in my hair...there is nothing so lovely as real flowers to wear." [4]

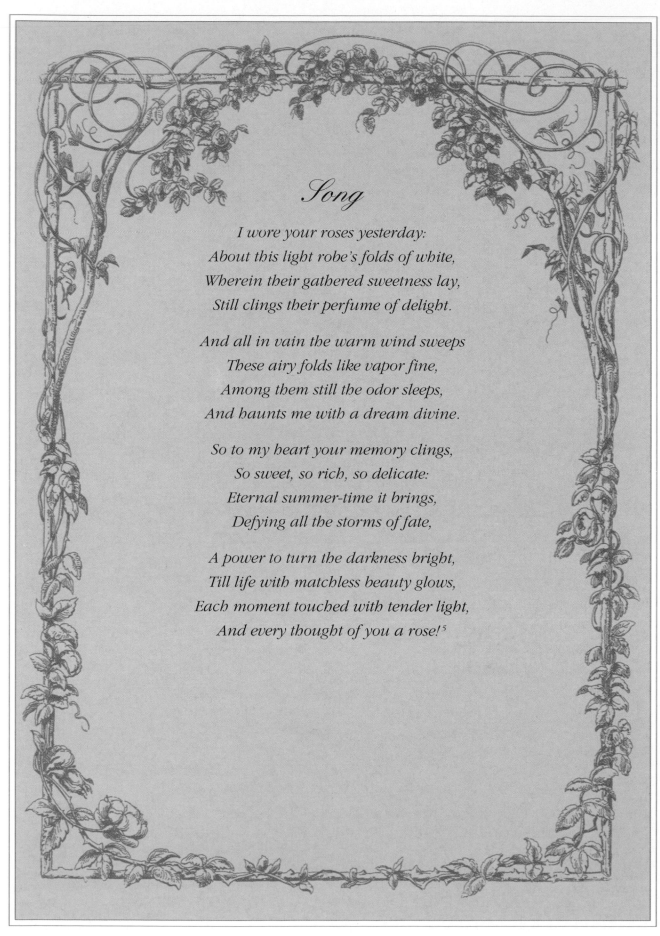

Song

I wore your roses yesterday:
About this light robe's folds of white,
Wherein their gathered sweetness lay,
Still clings their perfume of delight.

And all in vain the warm wind sweeps
These airy folds like vapor fine,
Among them still the odor sleeps,
And haunts me with a dream divine.

So to my heart your memory clings,
So sweet, so rich, so delicate:
Eternal summer-time it brings,
Defying all the storms of fate,

A power to turn the darkness bright,
Till life with matchless beauty glows,
Each moment touched with tender light,
And every thought of you a rose![5]

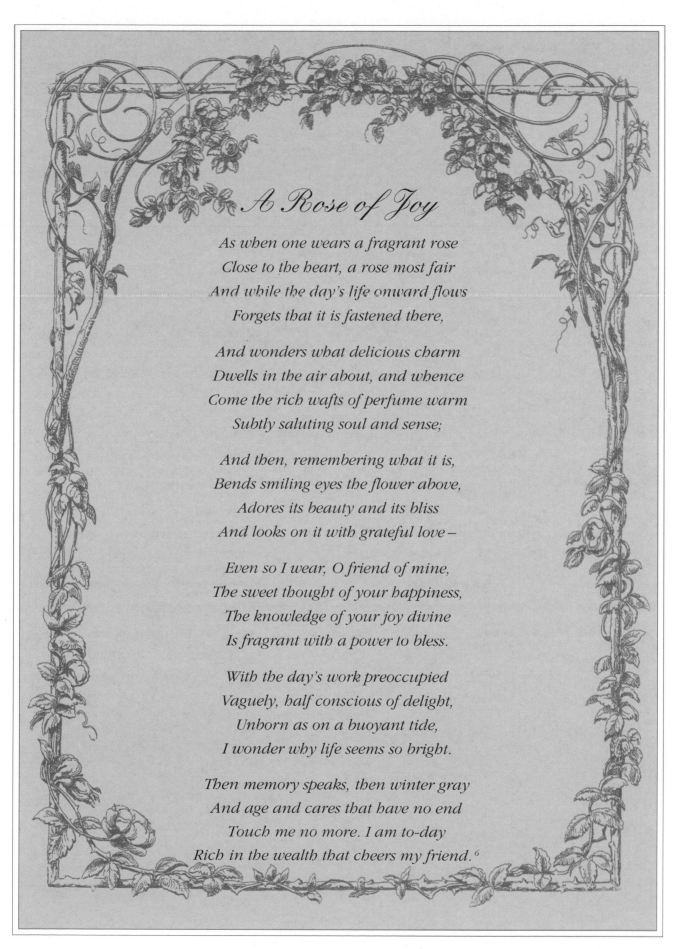

A Rose of Joy

As when one wears a fragrant rose
Close to the heart, a rose most fair
And while the day's life onward flows
Forgets that it is fastened there,

And wonders what delicious charm
Dwells in the air about, and whence
Come the rich wafts of perfume warm
Subtly saluting soul and sense;

And then, remembering what it is,
Bends smiling eyes the flower above,
Adores its beauty and its bliss
And looks on it with grateful love—

Even so I wear, O friend of mine,
The sweet thought of your happiness,
The knowledge of your joy divine
Is fragrant with a power to bless.

With the day's work preoccupied
Vaguely, half conscious of delight,
Unborn as on a buoyant tide,
I wonder why life seems so bright.

Then memory speaks, then winter gray
And age and cares that have no end
Touch me no more. I am to-day
Rich in the wealth that cheers my friend.[6]

A photograph of Celia in her early twenties served as a model for her inked profile in the center block of my quilt. The photograph was enlarged on a photocopier to size, and the profile then outlined with a marker. This outline was placed on a light box and traced on fabric with a pencil. Freezer paper was ironed to the wrong side of the fabric to stabilize it, and inking was done with a .01 black Pigma™ pen. With the photograph serving as a guide, more inked areas were added. When it was dry, the inked area was gently heat-set with an iron.

Celia's inked profile is set against a sunny blue sky fabric, like the immense sky visible from Celia's small island in the Atlantic – the same sky which, on beautiful sunny days, continues to make flowers in her gardens glow. As I carefully traced quilting lines outward from her profile, the lines reminded me of a sunrise, so I quilted them with gold metallic thread. Soon after, I came across these words written by Annie Fields about her dear friend Celia: *"The radiance of her nature was like an ever-rising sun of affection, constantly warming the hearts whereon it shone...."* [7] With these words in mind, I made the sunrise a dominant quilting motif for the rest of the quilt.

Celia's profile is encircled with a wreath of sculptured roses inspired by her love of roses and by two beautiful lines in a poem she wrote. The poem begins, *"I wore your roses yesterday"* and ends, *"And every thought of you a rose!"* [8]

In the language of flowers, *pink roses* symbolize grace and beauty; *red and white roses* creative force, joy, and unity; *rose-colored roses* shyness, beauty, pride, love; *shell-pink roses* youth, good health, and femininity. *Rosebuds* symbolize beauty and youth; *pink rosebuds* grace, beauty, and gentleness, a young girl; *red rosebuds* innocent hope, young and beautiful. Made in fabrics of all shades of rose and red, the sculptured roses in the wreath surrounding Celia's profile are meant to symbolize Celia's many, many virtues.

Celia's roses are more complicated to make than ribbon roses, but do not fear them, for they are beautiful. Because each petal is made individually, it takes about two hours to make a sculptured rose, but the results are well worth all the time and effort.

These sculptured roses are a variation of Helma Stewart's fabric roses, which I first saw in the spring 1991 issue of *American Quilter* magazine. I use a printed rose cut whole-cloth from chintz for the rose base, to give my rose realism. All the petals for this sculptured rose, as well as the buds and leaves, were also cut whole-cloth from chintz. The rose petals were lined with a hand-dyed silk by Maria McCormack Snyder, to add a touch of elegance.

CELIA'S SCULPTURED ROSE

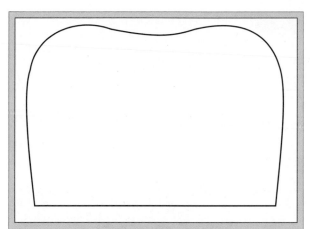

1 Using template plastic, make a master template from the petal outlined above.

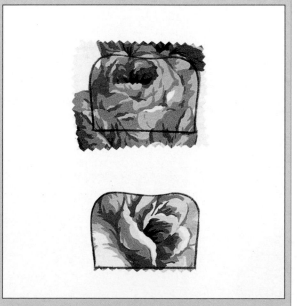

2 Select fabric for the petal backs. You may use various shades of rose, although I prefer to use a large-scale rose print for my petal choice. Trace the petal template on the fabric. This is your cutting line. Allow at least five petals per rose. Cut out each petal.

3 Place petals on petal-lining fabric and pin in place. I prefer to use a soft fabric for the petal linings, such as silk. Petal linings may be all the same shade or various shades for interest and excitement. A dyed silk with assorted shades of rose is ideal, however. Several pieces of lining can be used for variety.

4 Using a matching fine thread, stitch a row of tiny running stitches about ⅛ inch inside the curved edge of the petal. Leave the straight section open for the bottom of the petal. **Note:** This step may be stitched on a sewing machine in order to facilitate mass production of petals for many roses. It is also easier to sew petals onto a large piece of lining fabric, rather than cutting out individual petals.

5 Cut out the sewn petals from the lining.

8 Using a double thread in a matching color, whipstitch bottom opening closed. You now have a closed flat petal. Finish with a couple of overlapping stitches, but do not cut your thread.

6 Turn the petals inside out, and lightly finger press the curves.

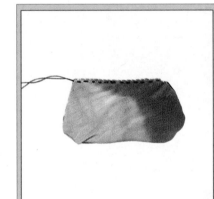

9 Run your needle and thread through the silk portion of the petal, right next to the whipstitching. Be careful not to go all the way through both layers of petal. You only want to stitch a row of running stitches through the silk or soft layer.

7 Turn raw edges of bottom in toward each other. Secure with a pin or two.

10 When you have stitched to the end of the petal bottom, gently pull the thread and gather the petal. Secure the thread with a couple of overlapping stitches, and cut your thread. You now have a curved, dimensional petal, which will enable you to "build" your rose in dimensional layers. Repeat the above steps for the remainder of your petals.

11 For the base of your sculptured rose, cut a printed rose from a piece of fabric with large-scale roses (the same fabric you used for the petals). Cut about ¼ inch beyond the rose print.

12 Make a fabric rosebud for the center unit of the rose. (My section on making rosebuds can give you helpful guidance.)

13 Select one of your separate petals to make the center unit.

14 Place a rosebud in the center of the petal, with the lining facing you. Attach the bud and petal pieces with several overlapping stitches at the gathering line of the bud.

15 Now begin to "build" your rose, one petal at a time. The curved petal's base slips easily under the center unit. Adjust this petal, turning a bit of its outer portion toward you to reveal some of the lining. When you are pleased with the arrangement, secure with a couple of hidden stitches through the back. (Sometimes I simply pin in place until I have all my petals arranged.)

16 Continue arranging petals on alternate sides of the center unit. End with the fifth or last petal in front of the center unit. Secure all the petals to the base rose fabric. Do not be concerned if most of the fabric base is hidden. Its main purpose is to serve as a base for petal attachment. Stitch the completed rose to the background fabric, turning under the outer edge of the rose to the desired final shape.

Sculptured rose completed. Optional step: Base may be lightly stuffed if it appears too flat in comparison to the dimensional petals.

Duck Island
Kittery Point, Maine
Shag Rock
Portsmouth
Grave
Mingo Rock
Siren's Cove
Celia Thaxter Cottage
Rye NH
Isles of Shoals
Babb's Cove
Broad Cove
Appledore Island
Atlantic Ocean
Lunging (Londoner's) Island
Smuttynose Island
Gosport Harbor
Square Rock
Half-Way Rocks
Cedar Island
Star Island
N
Seavey's Island
White Island
White I. Light
White I. Ledge
Isles of Shoals

Block Two:

Isles of Shoals Map

Celia's Enchanted New England Isles

"Very sad they look,
stern, bleak, and unpromising,
yet are they enchanted islands."[1]

Celia Thaxter
Among the Isles of Shoals

Featured Flower:

Lilies of the Valley,

Instructions

p. 31

ATLANTIC Ocean

Duck Island

Smuttynose

Cedar Island

Appledore

Star Island

MAINE
NEW HAMPSHIRE

Londoner's

Seavey's Island

White Island
LIGHTHOUSE

Maine
York
Kittery
Portsmouth
Greenland
Rye
The Isles
salisbury
Newburyport
N.H.
M.A.S.S.
Gloucester
Newbanville
BOSTON

THE ISLES of SHOALS

A part of early New England history, the Isles of Shoals were in 1614 visited by Englishman Captain John Smith, who found the islands so remarkable that he mapped them and re-named them Smith's Isles, though they continued to be called Isles of Shoals locally. Smith's vivid descriptions contributed to their early settlement.

Over 250 years later, Celia Thaxter would describe these remarkable islands and be responsible for their re-settlement. In her book *Among the Isles of Shoals*, she describes these islands located ten miles out of Portsmouth Harbor, which are called the Isles of Shoals "not because of the ragged reefs that run out beneath the water in all directions, ready to wreck and destroy, but because of the 'shoaling' or 'schooling,' of fish about them, which, in the mackerel and herring seasons, is remarkable...."[2]

Celia explains that the islands, varying in number from six to eight depending on the level of the tide, may appear as isolated barren rocks in the Atlantic Ocean, but are more than just rocks. An eloquent interpreter of the enchantment of the Isles of Shoals, Celia writes in *Among the Isles of Shoals*: "Landing for the first time, the stranger is struck only by the sadness of the place, – the vast loneliness; for there are not even trees to whisper with familiar voices, – nothing but sky and rocks. But the very wildness and desolation reveal a strange beauty to him....He sleeps with all the waves of the Atlantic murmuring in his ears, and wakes to the freshness of a

Opposite page: Map of Isles of Shoals and coastline. Inked by Andrew Labanaris. This area represented Celia's world. Except for one trip to Europe in 1880, Celia never traveled further south than Boston. She continually traveled back and forth from the Shoals to Newtonville and in later years Kittery Point, Maine.

Left: Isles of Shoals, Maine & New Hampshire by Peter Randall. Islands are L to R: Appledore, then Malaga, Smuttynose, Cedar, and Star all connected by a breakwater, White, Seavy's, Londoner's, and Duck Islands. As the state boundary between Maine and New Hampshire passes through the island group, Appledore, Smuttynose, and Duck Island are part of Maine, and the rest are considered part of New Hampshire.

summer morning; and it seems as if morning were made for the first time."[3]

Speaking of her beloved islands, Celia writes elsewhere in *Among the Isles of the Shoals*: "There is a strange charm about them, an indescribable influence in their atmosphere, hardly to be explained, but universally acknowledged. People forget the hurry and worry and fret of life after living there awhile...."[4]

These rocky islands where Celia spent much of her life were ever in her poetry, her prose, and her paintings. Her love of these Shoals provided inspiration for my quilt block

of the Isles, inked in permanent acid free ink, using the methods described for Block One.

Inking is not to be feared. If you can hold a pen and can write, you can ink a design such as this map. Simply work with a light touch of the pen to fabric. You can always darken your strokes if they are too light. If you are not sure of freehand art work, then lightly trace first with a pencil. Always use a mechanical hard-lead pencil rather than a wooden pencil, which may smudge and make too thick a line. Before too long, you will enjoy the process and the results!

Right: Isles of Shoals. *Photo courtesy of the University of New Hampshire, Dimond Library, Isles of Shoals Collection.*

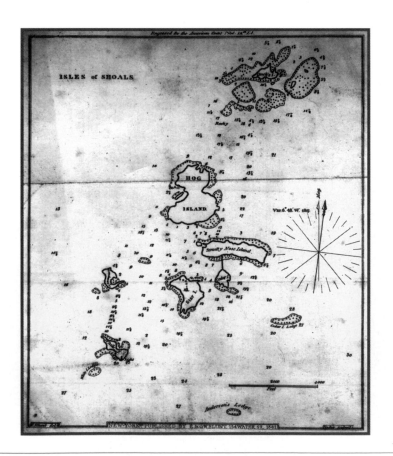

Instructions

LILIES OF THE VALLEY

Lilies of the valley symbolize the return of happiness, purity, and delicacy in the language of flowers. These lilies of the valley, which I've adapted from a design by Elly Sienkiewicz, symbolize the return of happiness that Celia felt each time she returned to the Isles of Shoals.

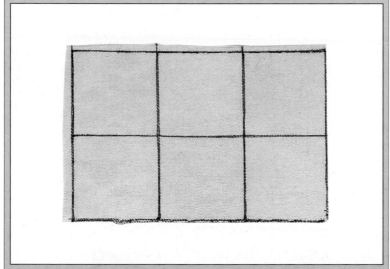

1 Cut 1 inch squares of white fabric using a rotary cutter or mark a grid with a pencil and cut with scissors.

3 Use a double length of white thread and stitch a row of tiny running stitches ⅛" in from the fringed edges. Leave the needle and thread attached.

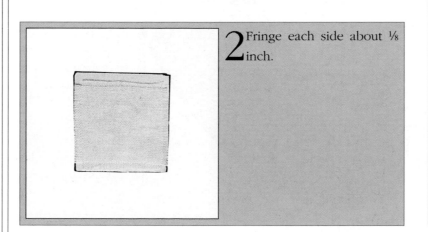

2 Fringe each side about ⅛ inch.

4 Fold the stitched square in half to form a triangle.

Reprinted by permission of C&T Publishing. Originally published in Elly Sienkiewicz's *Baltimore Beauties and Beyond, Pattern Companion to Vol. II for Dimensional Appliqué: Baskets, Blooms & Baltimore Borders.*

6 Gather tightly and secure with 2 or 3 overlapping stitches. Cut the loose thread.

5 Gently pull thread and gather the folded triangle into a pouch shape.

7 Position lilies of the valley along a curved, embroidered stem as shown in the lily diagram below. Attach the lily floret with an anchoring stitch through the top portion of the flower and add a second stitch through the gathered section. (See black lines in first floret in Step 5.)

8 Small stems from the floret to the main stem may be embroidered or inked. Add a gold bead or two at the ruffled edge.

Block Three:
Celia's Family Tree

The Laighton-Thaxter Legend Begins

Featured Flower:

Violets,

Instructions

p. 39

Vase of Violets,

Pattern

p. 38

"'You must have been very lonely at the light.'
They did not know that where our mother dwelt
there was happiness also.
I am sure no family was ever more united and contented than
the Laightons were on White Island."[1]

Oscar Laighton
Ninety Years at the Isles of Shoals

Born in 1805, Celia's father, Thomas B. Laighton, was the son of a prominent Portsmouth, New Hampshire shipping family. He longed for a life at sea, but lameness resulting from a childhood illness kept him on shore, where he became a very prosperous businessman, a politician, and a public-spirited citizen who was an eloquent orator. He highly valued books and schooling (his personal library is said to have contained over 1,000 volumes), and as a member of the Portsmouth School Board, he was instrumental in providing the first public library.

On June 23, 1831, Thomas married Eliza Rymes of Newington, New Hampshire, a true nineteenth century woman concerned foremost with her family's comfort and well being. This couple frequently entertained politicians and prominent community members, and Eliza demonstrated a wonderful gift for making people feel welcome and for cooking fine meals! It is said that Celia inherited her mother's charm.

Still longing for a life at sea,

Thomas purchased four of the Isles of Shoals off the coast of New Hampshire after Celia's birth. As far back as the sixteenth century, the Isles of Shoals had attracted scores of European fishermen, who visited the Shoals and returned to England with their holds full of fish, earning as much in seven months at the Shoals as in twenty months at another location.

Because of taxation, the fishing industry had declined after the Revolutionary War, but many fishermen were beginning to return to the Shoals in the early 1800's. Thomas hoped to use his connections in the shipping business to re-establish the once prosperous and very profitable fishing industry on the Isles of Shoals.

Frustrated by an unsuccessful bid for public office in Portsmouth, in 1839 Thomas decided to accept a two-year position of lighthouse keeper on White Island, Isles of Shoals. Thomas may have felt that he could use this time on the island to work to re-establish the fishing industry there. The Portsmouth community was shocked that Thomas, a prominent businessman and politician, would accept such a lowly job and move his entire family from the bustle of the port city to those barren islands! He officially assumed the position on October 1, 1839.

Though Celia was not yet five years old, she remembered well her first trip to White Island. Years later she would write this recollection in her first book of prose, *Among the Isles of Shoals*: "How delightful was that long, first sail to the Isles of Shoals! How pleasant the unaccustomed sound of the incessant ripple against the boat-side, the sight of the wide water and limitless sky, the warmth of the broad sunshine that made us blink like young sandpipers as we sat in triumph, perched among the household goods with which the little craft was laden."[2]

Celia, her mother, and Celia's brother, Oscar, who had been born only three months earlier, arrived on White Island on October 3, 1839, joining Thomas, who had arrived one week earlier with the furniture. Though only a babe during the actual voyage, Oscar had often heard the story of his first sea voyage from his parents. He recollected the experience in his book *Ninety Years at the Isles of Shoals*: "I have often thought of my blessed mother leaving the safety of the mainland for the dangers of the far spread Atlantic and making her home on the wave-swept islands, yet I know she forgot all fear in her beautiful devotion to father and her children."[3]

Although the Laightons were the only household on the island, their isolation from the mainland did not seem to bother them. Celia's years on White Island proved to be among the happiest in her life. Her family developed very close bonds which would hold tight through all their lives. The Laightons were alone on White Island, but they were not lonely, and there was much sunshine in their lives.

Less is more seemed an appropriate design concept for the family

history block to be included in my tribute to Celia Thaxter. A simple tree against a blue sky was used as the background on which to ink the Laighton-Thaxter descendants. Unique fabrics were used to add details. A hand-painted muted green became the tree's foliage. Marbleized browns provided perfect bark. The hand-dyed sky fabric used here appeared throughout the quilt in almost every block.

A wreath of oak leaves and acorns symbolizing longevity surrounds Celia's Family Tree block. A cut-work wreath (pattern #6 from Elly Sienkiewicz's *Baltimore Beauties*

and Beyond series, Volume II, C & T Publishing, p. 117) surrounds the entire design. The symbolism of this wreath was appropriate for Celia's spirit, which has never died in over 100 years. Sun rays against the blue sky are quilted with gold metallic thread. The foliage of the tree is quilted in an oak leaf pattern with gold metallic thread to represent sunshine.

Instructions follow for making ribbon renditions of the violets that grow on the hilltop graves on Appledore, where the Laighton family and Celia Thaxter are buried. They remain together as a family even in death.

LAIGHTON – THAXTER FAMILY TREE

THOMAS B. LAIGHTON (1805 – 1866)
MARRIED 1831 PORTSMOUTH, NH
ELIZA RYMES (1804 – 1877)
 BORN
 1. HELEN (D. AT 11 MOS.)
 2. CELIA (B. JUNE 29, 1835, PORTSMOUTH, NH)
 (D. AUGUST 26, 1894, APPLEDORE I)
  MARRIED SEPTEMBER 30, 1857
  LEVI LINCOLN THAXTER (1821 – 1884)
   1. KARL (1852 – 1912)
   2. JOHN (1854 – 1928)
    MARRIED TO MARY STODDARD 1886
    1. ROSAMOND (1895 – 1989)
   3. ROLAND (1858 – 1923)
    MARRIED TO MABEL (MARY) FREEMAN 1886
    1. CHARLES ELIOT
    2. KATHERINE
    3. EDMUND
    4. BETTY
 3. OSCAR (1839 – 1939)
 4. CEDRIC (1840 – 1899)
  MARRIED TO JULIA STOWELL 1881
   1. MARGARET
    MARRIED EDWARD FORBES [DATE UNKNOWN]
   2. BARBARA
   3. RUTH

Left: Inked details for *Laighton – Thaxter Family tree.*

5 Attach the petals to themselves, with a couple of overlapping stitches, to form a complete circle. Pull the center together with needle and thread. The center will be slightly open. Attach the flower to background fabric with stitches through the center.

6 Heavily bead the center area to camouflage all raw edges. Outer wired petals may be "sculpted" or folded over themselves toward the center to form a turned edge.

Block Four:

The Lighthouse

Celia's Lighthouse Years

"I well remember my first sight of White Island, where we took up our abode on leaving the mainland…It was at sunset in autumn that we set ashore on that loneliest, lovely rock, where the lighthouse looked down on us like some tall, black-capped giant, and filled me with awe and wonder…The stars were beginning to twinkle; the wind blew cold, charged with the sea's sweetness; the sound of many waters half bewildered me. Some one began to light the lamps in the tower. Rich red and golden, they swung round in mid-air; everything was strange and fascinating and new." [1]

Celia Thaxter
Among the Isles of Shoals

Featured Flower:

Calendulas,

Instructions

p. 47

White island was large enough for only the lighthouse and a cottage, connected by a covered walkway over a rocky chasm. Soon after landing, Celia and her family entered the cottage that was to become their home. Celia later comments: "A blissful home the little house became to the children who entered it that quiet evening...I do not think a happier triad ever existed than we were, living in that profound isolation. It takes so little to make a healthy child happy." [2]

A biographer says of Celia's parents and their "temporary" relocation to the White Island: "It could never have occurred to either of them that they were leading these children through a fairyland into an island kingdom where Celia would reign as queen." [3]

Young Celia's years on White Island were filled with simple adventures and wonder at the miracles of nature. Years later she would write "The Wreck of the Pocahontas," a poem describing a bitter storm during their first winter. Helpless to do

anything, the family watched a ship flounder and wreck. Survival on the island drew them together and gave them an inner strength that would sustain them the rest of their lives.

It was Eliza who most held the family together. She had the courageous spirit needed to bring up three small children on a small rocky island 10 miles from the nearest port. Devoted to her family, she filled their home with sunshine, even during the long, cold, and dark months of New England winter. Oscar writes of his mother: "In all the world, there could be no one so sweet....Her charm was her interest in and instant sympathy with all to whom she talked. To know her for even five minutes made even a stranger her friend. Mother...was affectionately called Aunt Eliza by everyone."[4]

Thomas Laighton provided an education for Celia, Oscar, and Cedric. Celia quickly absorbed all he taught her and never lost a moment she could give to study. Thomas brought his large personal library to the lighthouse from Portsmouth and read literary classics aloud to the

family every evening in their cottage kitchen, which was filled with blooming plants and Thomas's singing canaries.

Oscar remembers these winter evenings by the fire. "I can recall… our cozy kitchen with all the family gathered round the fire…while outside the sea was thundering against White Island Head with a force that rattled the dishes in the closet." [5]

As lighthouse keeper, Thomas was responsible for keeping the lanterns burning. The White Island lighthouse had first been erected in 1820. With its tower of stone and lantern 90 feet above the tide, its light was visible for 21 miles. A new tower built 45 years later in 1865 still stands today.

The lighthouse lantern had to be watched all night, so Thomas could not do this job alone. He had a helper from the mainland, Ben Whaling, with whom he worked the lighthouse in four-hour shifts, to keep the lantern revolving. As the oldest child, Celia soon learned to help with the care of the lantern, keeping its windows shining and its reflectors polished.

Flowers were very scarce on White Island and Celia treasured every one she saw, probably inheriting that love from her mother, who year-round made flowers a part of her life. Celia's first garden was planted that first spring on White Island, when she was five years old: "I had a scrap of garden, literally not more than a yard square, wherein grew only African marigolds rich in color as barbaric gold…." [6]

The yellow flowers she describes are pot marigolds or calendulas. She would continue to plant these flowers, in later years as a tribute to the poet John Greenleaf Whittier, who had admired them in her gardens and had spent many happy times visiting Celia on the Isles of Shoals. [7]

Right: Aerial view of White Island Light. Photo: Peter Randall, Portsmouth, NH.

The Lighthouse Block

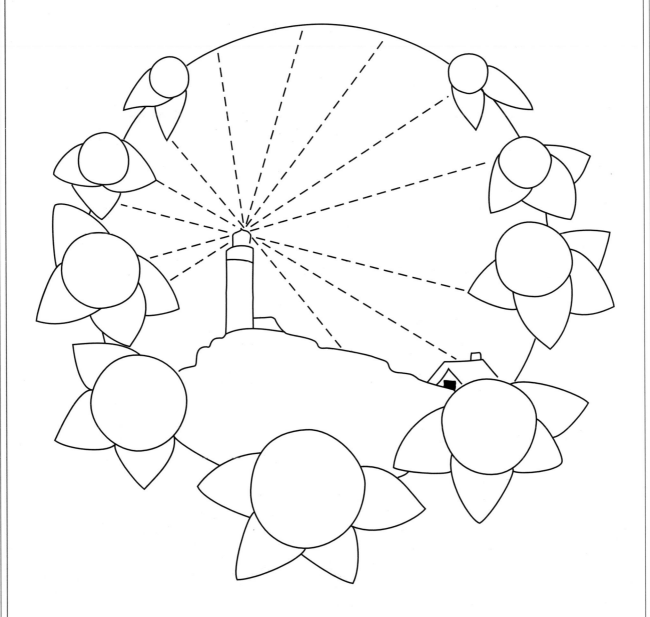

The Lighthouse block is reduced 80% to fit the page. Enlarge by 125% to reproduce full-size.

For my block on the Lighthouse Years, Celia's vivid description of her arrival on White Island provided the design inspiration. To translate Celia's words into fabric, I first selected fabric appropriate for her sunset description. A piece of hand-painted fabric by Mickey Lawler/ Skydyes made the perfect sky. The fabrics for rock, water, and the lighthouse quickly came together.

I used a photograph for a silhouette tracing of the lighthouse, cottage, and island. I enlarged the tracing on a photocopier, traced the outline onto freezer paper, cut the shape out, and ironed it onto the fabric, to provide the sewing guide.

The background space was quilted with golden rays from the lighthouse lantern. The wreath of yellow flowers surrounding the lighthouse block represents Celia's first garden planted that first spring on White Island when she was five years old, the one with only calendulas – "African marigolds, rich in color as barbaric gold...." [8]

My calendulas (pot marigolds) fashioned after the ones Celia grew at age five, were made from wired ribbon, which I overdyed with a deep shade of yellow and a pearlescence for a sparking sunlight effect.

CALENDULAS

In the language of flowers, calendulas symbolize health, joy, remembrance, the sun, and affection.

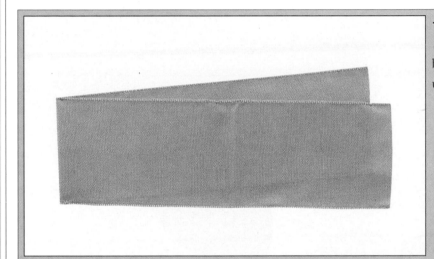

1 Use 12 inches of 1½ inch wide yellow wire-edged ribbon per flower. (More may be used for a fuller flower.)

2 Use a 36-inch piece of thread in a matching color, doubled and knotted. Stitch a row of running stitches through the center of the ribbon's length.

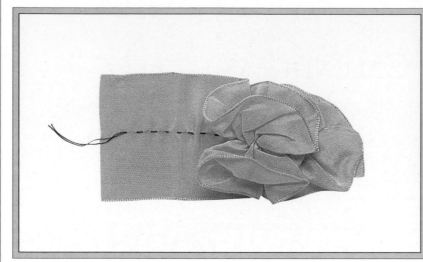

3 Every few inches, gently pull the thread and gather the ribbon. The ribbon will twist around itself. Do not wait until the end to gather the ribbon. The thread may twist and break and you will have to start over again.

4 When you have stitched to the end of the ribbon and gathered the ribbon fairly tightly, end your stitches with a couple of overlapping stitches. Cut the thread. Tuck the cut edges of the ribbon ends underneath the flower and tack to the flower's center. Anchor the flower to your background fabric with a few hidden stitches through the center of the flower.

Block Five:

Sandpiper

The Carefree Days of Youth

*"With the first warm days we built our
little mountains of wet gravel on the beach,
and danced after the sandpipers
at the edge of the foam...."* [1]

Celia Thaxter
Among the Isles of Shoals

Featured Flower:

Five-petal Roses,

Instructions

p. 55

Celia's writing tells of happy childhood years spent on White Island (1839–1847). Celia and her brothers knew every inch of their island home, and endlessly enjoyed the blessings of Mother Nature. They "launched fleets of purple mussel-shells on the still pools in the rocks, left by the tide, pools that were like bits of fallen rainbows with the wealth of the sea." [2]

White Island was little more than a barren rock with sparse vegetation that grew among the rocks, so Celia noticed every flower and blade of grass. She recalls: "I remember in the spring kneeling on the ground to seek the first blades of grass that pricked through the soil and bringing them into the house to study and wonder over. Better than a shop full of toys they were to me!" [3] This love of nature would never leave Celia, who wondered in awe how "every flower knew what to do and to be." [4] She once commented: "All flowers had for me such human interest, they were so dear and precious I hardly liked to gather them and when they were withered, I carried them all to one place and laid them tenderly together, and never liked to pass the spot where they were hidden." [5]

Enjoying fully a perfect summer day, Celia wrote: "...when I went out to milk the little cow, it was hardly possible to go further than the doorstep, for pure wonder, as I looked abroad...." At another time, she has commented, "Infinite variety of beauty always awaited me, and filled me with as absorbing, unrea-

Right: Detail of *A TRIBUTE TO CELIA THAXTER,* upper right corner of quilt, featuring song sparrows and nest in morning-glory vine.

soning joy such as makes the song-sparrows sing,…a sense of perfect bliss. Coming back in the sunshine, the morning glories would lift up their faces, all awake, to my adoring gaze…It seemed as if they had gathered the peace of the golden morning in their still depths even as my heart had gathered it." [6]

When the tides were right, the children would explore neighboring Seavy's Island, which was connected to White Island by a sandbar exposed only at low tide. Oscar recalls: "Often when the tide was low, sister would take us across to Seavey's Island, where in summer we found a few wild flowers. On this island many sandpipers had their nests, but not for worlds would we disturb them." [7]

Years later, the sandpipers' antics inspired Celia to write one of her best remembered poems, "Sandpiper." Included in *McGuffy's Fourth Reader*, it was read and loved by school children everywhere. Author and friend Sarah Orne Jewett often called Celia by the pet name Sandpiper.

This famous poem by Celia, several of her comments on sandpipers, her love of roses, and a line drawing completed by my son at age 16 were the inspirations for my Sandpiper block, which was one of the easier blocks to design. A piece of antique lace was used as sea foam on the shore, and the sandpiper was stitched as layered appliqué with inked feathers and other details. The legs and beak were embroidered for added texture.

The roses, of course, were the beach roses that grew on the island. *Rosa rugosa* are simple, five-petal roses. I used a hand-painted rose colored fabric and tie-dyed raw silk for the gathered petals. Realistic printed leaves were cut from fabric and placed randomly around the roses to serve as the base for the wreath of roses.

Golden rays of sunshine were quilted in the background sky.

The Sandpiper

Across the narrow beach we flit,
One little sandpiper and I,
And fast I gather, bit by bit,
The scattered driftwood bleached and dry.
The wild waves reach their hands for it,
The wild wind raves, the tide runs high,
As up and down the beach we flit–
One little sandpiper and I.

Above our heads the sullen clouds
Scud black and swift across the sky,
Like silent ghosts in misty shrouds
Stand out the white lighthouses high.
Almost as far as eye can reach
I see the close-reefed vessels fly,
As fast we flit along the beach,–
One little sandpiper and I.

I watch him as he skims along,
Uttering his sweet and mournful cry.
He starts not at my fitful song,
Or flash of fluttering drapery.
He has no thought of any wrong,
He scans me with a fearful eye.
Stanch friends are we, well tried and strong,
The little sandpiper and I.

Comrade, where wilt thou be to-night
When the loosed storm breaks furiously?
My driftwood fire will burn so bright!
To what warm shelter canst thou fly?
The tempest rushed through the sky.
For are we not God's children both,

Thou, little sandpiper and I? [8]

The Sandpiper Block

The Sandpiper block is reduced 80% to fit the page. Enlarge by 125% to reproduce full-size.

FIVE-PETAL ROSES

Roses symbolize grace, beauty, love, joy, and friendship. These five-petal beach roses are fabric versions of those growing wild on the islands.

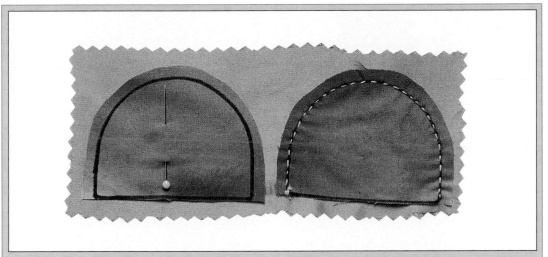

1 Two pieces of fabric are needed for each seamed and turned petal. I prefer a cotton for the outer portion for stability and a silk or silk-like fabric for petal lining. Make a template from the petal above. Trace this petal onto the wrong side of the cotton fabric. This is the cutting line. Cut out five petals.

2 Place the cut petals on the silk fabric for the petal lining. Pin in place. Stitch ⅛ inch from the curved line with tiny running stitches in matching thread. This step can be done on the sewing machine. Leave the bottom straight edge open.

3 Cut out the petals. Turn them inside out, and gently finger press into shape. Using double thread, stitch the open edges together ⅛ inch from the cut edge.

4 Gather as tightly as possible. Secure with two or three over-lapping stitches and cut the thread. Make four more petals.

5 Attach petals to each other, one at a time. Overlap each approximately by one-third. Secure to each other with 2 or 3 overlapping stitches. Continue in this manner until all five petals are attached and form a complete circle.

6 To form the yellow-fringed center, cut 36 inches of yellow embroidery floss and fold several times until about 2 inches long. Wrap through the center with saved wire from ribbon roses or use thread. Fold center unit in half and wrap wire or thread around base to form a tuft of floss. Trim off excess floss to about 1 inch in length. Insert into center of rose. Attach with a few stitches in the back of the rose.

7 Realistic fabric leaves may be added. Select leaves from a piece of fabric with printed leaves. Cut beyond the leaf about ⅛ inch to ¼ inch. Position under the rose and needle-turn any raw edges under. Use the leaf print as a stitching guide.

Block Six:

The "Pinafore"

a pretty sight the little vessel down the beautiful Piscotaqua like a Mayday procession

Levi Thaxter Enters Celia's Life

*"How patient have I been,
Sitting alone, a happy little maid,
Waiting to see, careless and unafraid,
My father's boat come in..."* [1]

Celia Thaxter
The Poems of Celia Thaxter

Featured Flower:

Sweet Peas,

Instructions

p. 65

Right: Smuttynose Island. Photo courtesy of the University of New Hampshire, Dimond Library, Isles of Shoals Collection.

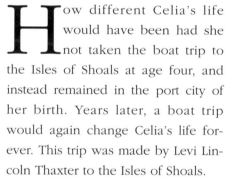

How different Celia's life would have been had she not taken the boat trip to the Isles of Shoals at age four, and instead remained in the port city of her birth. Years later, a boat trip would again change Celia's life forever. This trip was made by Levi Lincoln Thaxter to the Isles of Shoals.

Though Thomas Laighton was keeper of White Island Light, he had not completely given up his business and political interests. When he was elected to the Board of Selectmen in Portsmouth in 1841, his family had no desire to return to the mainland, so he moved them into the Haley house on Smuttynose Island, which allowed him to make frequent trips to Portsmouth to fulfill his political duties. The lighthouse position was temporarily filled by another keeper.

Smuttynose, much larger than White Island, was an inviting and intriguing island to the Laighton children. It had once been the haunt of smugglers and pirates, and even had a ghost! It also had a hotel for summer boarders built by Captain Samuel Haley, who had settled on the island shortly before the Revolutionary War and done much to improve the island for its inhabitants.

While on White Island Thomas and Eliza had often entertained visitors from the mainland, which gave them experience and confidence as potential innkeepers. Once settled on Smuttynose, Thomas decided to dust off the old sign on Captain Haley's hotel and reopen the Mid-Ocean House of Entertainment. He and Eliza became innkeepers and Thomas' dream of making his fortune in the hotel business began to become reality.

At the conclusion of his political term, Thomas moved his family back to White Island for another two-year term as lighthouse keeper, during which time he continued to make improvements on the Smuttynose hotel. He often sailed to Smuttynose twice a day to oversee the work, twice making the difficult landing on White Island. Celia often sat for hours on the rocks waiting for her father's return, holding a lantern to guide him to safe landing. In later years she wrote of this in her poem "Watching."

On July 24, 1846, Levi Lincoln Thaxter arrived on White Island. This man's arrival would change the course of life at the islands and give them a whole new importance in American history.[2] Born in 1821 to one of Massachusetts' oldest and most distinguished families, Levi was

a Harvard graduate with a law degree, who had recently been floundering in search of a profession. He didn't want to practice law, and his study of acting in New York City had proved unsuccessful. Family arguments over Levi's activity led to a nervous breakdown and a friend's recommendation that Levi travel to the Isles of Shoals to recuperate. Learning many Boston physicians were sending patients to the Shoals for its healthy climate, Levi took the advice.

Levi was charmed by the islands and impressed with Thomas Laighton's ambitious dreams of reviving the fishing industry and developing the islands as a summer resort. Thomas' hotel was doing well, and he wanted to build a much larger one on Hog Island.

Levi was certain others would be

as attracted to these enchanting islands as he was. The "Brothers and Sisters," a group of young college-age people with whom Levi associated in Newton, Massachusetts, would surely love the place. They gathered regularly to discuss life and literature, reading the newest works by Emerson, Browning, Tennyson, and Longfellow as rapidly as they were published. If these young people destined to become an important part of literary society by the late nineteenth century were to discover the Isles of Shoals, it could be the making of the islands. Levi's first visit to the islands lasted almost one month, and he visited again in April of the following year.

Thomas began to draw up plans for the hotel on Hog Island. Acting on impulse, he invited Levi out for a third visit with the intention of proposing a partnership. Levi arrived and enthusiastically joined in partnership with Thomas in his new hotel. He returned to the island a week later with $2,500 from his father for a half interest in the Hog Island and became a partner on Sept. 10, 1847.

Levi returned in October 1847, invited by Thomas, to spend the winter while they were building the hotel on Appledore Island. (Thomas had changed Hog Island's name back to its original name, Appledore.) Since he was so busy with the many details of building the hotel that he no longer had time for his children's education, Thomas hired Levi to tutor the children. Oscar recalls his mother's being "delighted that her children were having the benefit of this heaven-sent school." [3]

Celia was in awe of Levi's worldliness and his vast knowledge of poetry and literature. He soon recognized that Celia possessed unusual intellect and introduced her to a new world of contemporary poets. As Celia blossomed into a young beauty, their innocent mutual admiration grew into something more. Levi was falling in love with 12-year-old Celia, though he was 14 years older than she.

The winter quickly passed, spring came, and with it, the completion of the Appledore Hotel, which opened to the public on June 15, 1848. Its first season was successful and Thomas was very pleased. By the following year, however, Levi realized that the hotel business was not for him.

Thomas bought out Levi's share of the hotel and the island. Levi retained the North Cottage where he continued to stay and received many visits from his Boston friends and family. Levi had grown to be so much a part of the Laighton family that he was taken for granted as an older brother, friend, and teacher to the children, a junior partner to Thomas, a son to Eliza.

All this changed when Levi fell in love with Celia and wanted to marry her. Thomas was not ready for Levi's proposal of marriage in November 1848. Celia was only 13 years old. Thomas flew into a rage and ordered Levi off the island. Levi responded that he would live on the island until Celia was old enough to speak for herself. In February, Thomas reluctantly consented to the

Right: Celia at age 15 at the time of her engagement to Levi. Photo courtesy of the University of New Hampshire, Dimond Library, Isles of Shoals Collection.

wedding, if Levi and Celia would wait 12 months. Celia enrolled in the Mt. Washington Female Seminary in South Boston; she stayed with Levi's family in Watertown, MA.

Eliza was pleased, Oscar and Cedric were delighted, but in Watertown the news of Levi's engagement must have echoed through every parlor and kitchen. Levi, the eligible bachelor with two degrees from Harvard and generations of culture behind him, was engaged to a mere child with no education, whose father was a lighthouse keeper and amateur hotel man on a barren island.[4]

Oscar fondly remembers the evening Celia told him of her engagement to Levi, saying, "Goodbye sweet day," a phrase which became the title of a poem written about this sunset.[5]

The summer of 1851 was filled with excitement for Celia. She became engaged to Levi. The hotel had just opened, and guests were arriving daily including many of Levi's friends from Boston. They spent many happy hours in his cottage reading the poetry of Tennyson, Browning, Emerson, Longfellow, Hawthorne, and Whittier, reading their own verses, listening to music, and discussing social issues.

Celia was very much a part of this very stimulating scene and she would continue this tradition of stimulating conversation and readings later, with gatherings of authors and musicians in her own parlor on Appledore. Celia's already full life had been much enriched by the fateful arrival of Levi Thaxter in 1846.

To create my tribute to the Pinafore's arrival, I turned to Celia's words for inspiration. A photograph of the Pinafore provided a model for the inked block. Photocopy enlargements of the Pinafore photo enabled me to get just the right scale for the block. I only had to select fabric for the sea and the dock. All other details were be inked and/or embroidered.

For the sea I choose a piece of marbleized fabric made by Mary R. Ryan Designs. I used a window template to select just the right fabric section, to give the illusion of waves. Embroidery and inking created the baskets filled with seedlings on the wooded dock, also made from marbleized fabric to resemble wood. The ocean is quilted with silver thread in a Clamshell design.

The sky has a golden sunrise quilted with golden metallic thread. A free hanging braided cord of embroidery floss "ties" the boat to the dock with a three-dimensional effect. The wreath of spring flowers and buds is taken from the cutwork block in a book by Elly Sienkiewicz (*Baltimore Beauties and Beyond, Vol. I – Pattern Companion*, C & T Publishing, pattern #37, p. 78). Included on this block are inked flower details of stamens and pollen around each flower.

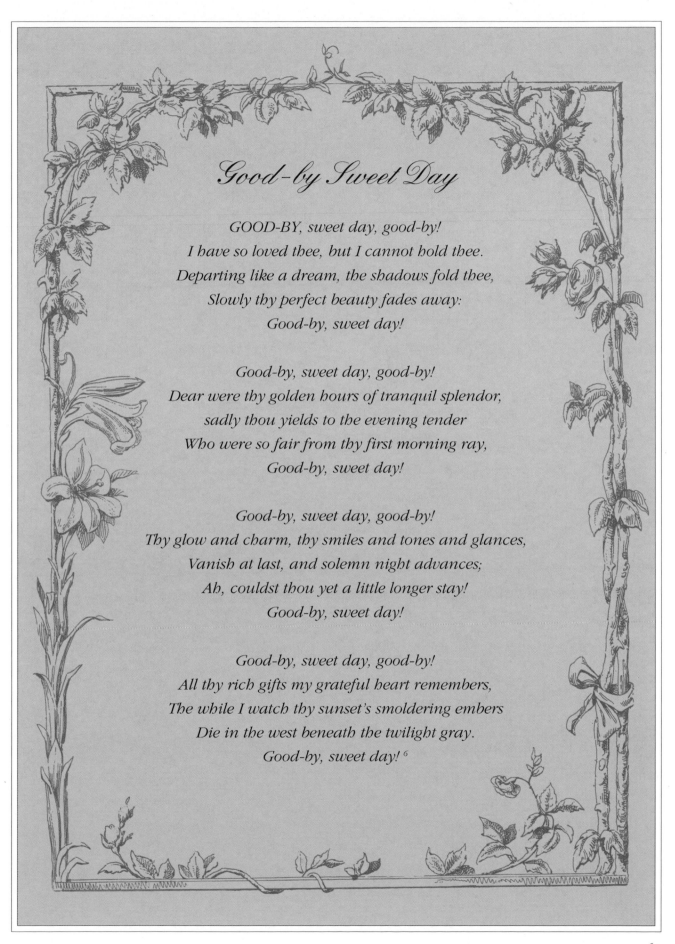

Good-by Sweet Day

GOOD-BY, sweet day, good-by!
I have so loved thee, but I cannot hold thee.
Departing like a dream, the shadows fold thee,
Slowly thy perfect beauty fades away:
Good-by, sweet day!

Good-by, sweet day, good-by!
Dear were thy golden hours of tranquil splendor,
sadly thou yields to the evening tender
Who were so fair from thy first morning ray,
Good-by, sweet day!

Good-by, sweet day, good-by!
Thy glow and charm, thy smiles and tones and glances,
Vanish at last, and solemn night advances;
Ah, couldst thou yet a little longer stay!
Good-by, sweet day!

Good-by, sweet day, good-by!
All thy rich gifts my grateful heart remembers,
The while I watch thy sunset's smoldering embers
Die in the west beneath the twilight gray.
Good-by, sweet day! [6]

"Pinafore" Block

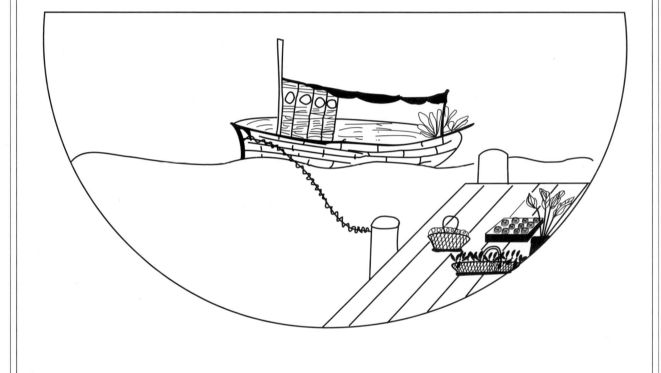

Instructions

SWEET PEAS

Sweet peas symbolize delicate pleasures and departures. These sweet peas represent those in the bouquet of sweet peas that Celia would carry on her wedding day.

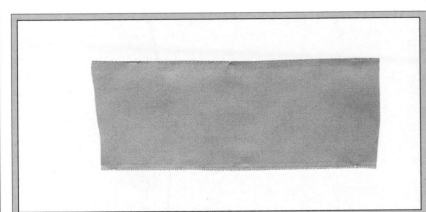

1 For each flower, cut 4 inches of 1½ inch wide wire-edged ribbon in soft colors such as pink, rose, coral, or white.

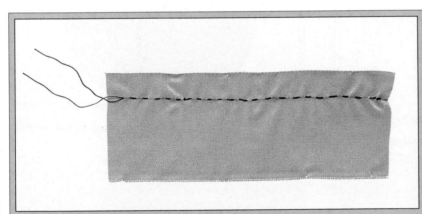

2 Cut 36 inches of matching thread, doubled and knotted. Stitch a row of running stitches ½ inch down from the wired selvage edge along the length of the ribbon as shown.

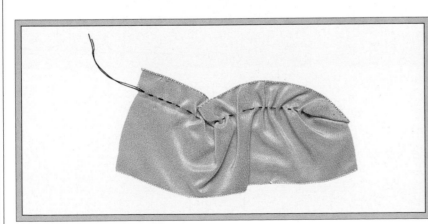

3 Gather as tightly as possible and secure with 2 or 3 over-lapping stitches.

4 Spread open flower, as indicated above.

5 Fold ribbon together so that cut edges are matching. Stitch a narrow seam stopping at the gathered edge. This seam will become the back of the flower. Leave the top ½ inch section unseamed.

6 Fold the top gathered edge over the wider bottom section. Be sure the raw edges do not show.

7 Arrange each of the sweet peas alternately on an embroidered stem. Attach to background fabric with hidden stitches. Add tendrils to the stems (inked or embroidered).

Block Seven:

The Hotel

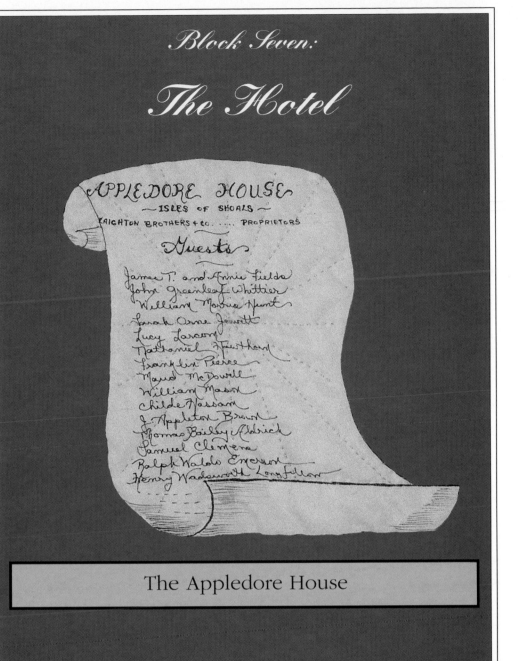

APPLEDORE HOUSE
~ ISLES OF SHOALS ~
LAIGHTON BROTHERS & CO. ..... PROPRIETORS

Guests

James T. and Annie Fields
John Greenleaf Whittier
William Morris Hunt
Sarah Orne Jewitt
Lucy Larcom
Nathaniel Hawthorn
Franklin Pierce
Maud McDowell
William Mason
Childe Hassam
J. Appleton Brown
Thomas Bailey Aldrich
Samuel Clemens
Ralph Waldo Emerson
Henry Wadsworth Longfellow

The Appledore House

*"The remarkable people who came to us added greatly
to the charm of the place. Here gathered the culture
and talent of all New England, but at this time we did not
realize the great privilege we were enjoying."* [1]

Oscar Laighton
Ninety Years on the Isles of Shoals

Vase of Roses,

Pattern

p. 74

Featured Flower:

Full-blown

Ribbon Roses

Instructions

p. 75

Ribbon Leaves,

Instructions

p. 79

At first, visitors came for day trips, curious to see "the place Laighton built." After tasting Eliza's wonderful cooking and breathing in the refreshing sea air, they returned to stay longer, promising future visits. Word of the new hotel spread, and more and more guests came.

The family awaited each arriving boat and listened for the toot of the boat's whistle, which passengers thought was a welcome ashore toot. In reality, the number of times the whistle was tooted told the family how many extra quarts of water needed to be added to the chowder to accommodate the arriving lunch crowd!

A September 2, 1848 article in the *New Hampshire Journal* described a visit made to Appledore during its first season: "We soon sighted Appledore Island with the newly built Appledore House....Waiting to receive us stood our hospitable friend Mr. Thaxter the genuine specimen of a gentleman. We wonder why a gentleman of his accomplishments, a graduate of Harvard, should be content to settle on this barren remote island? He told us that during the summer one day there were 98 guests from all parts of the Northeastern states! They come hungry and go away with satisfied appetite, come feeble and go away strong, come pale and sick and return florid and healthy, come full of cash and return with scarcely a 'Picayune.' "[2]

Many famous guests came to the Appledore House over the years, including such artists, musicians, and writers as Thomas Bailey Aldrich, Henry Ward Beecher, Ole Bull, Samuel Clemens, Richard Henry Dana, Childe Hassam, Nathaniel Hawthorne, William Dean Howells, William Morris Hunt, Samuel Longfellow, James Russell Lowell, Harriet Beecher Stowe, Sarah Orne Jewett, Lucy Larcom, James and Annie Fields, John Greenleaf Whittier, and Frances H. Burnett (whose Little Lord Fauntleroy was inspired by Cedric Laighton). Initially such notable people came to the Shoals

Right: The Appledore House first opened to the public on June 15, 1848, less than one year after the ground breaking. The long isolated Laighton family eagerly awaited their first guests, brought by a small schooner chartered by the hotel to bring passengers to the Isles. Cedric (left) and Oscar behind the registration desk. Photo circa 1880. Photo courtesy of the University of New Hampshire, Dimond Library, Isles of Shoals Collection.

Left: Appledore House, first stage. Photo courtesy of the University of New Hampshire, Dimond Library, Isles of Shoals Collection.

Left: By 1874 the Appledore House was really bustling and considered a fine hotel fulfilling guests' every need. Photo courtesy of the University of New Hampshire, Dimond Library, Isles of Shoals Collection.

Left: Appledore House in its prime. Though the Appledore House could accommodate five hundred guests, Oscar Laighton recalls the hotel: "...often found it difficult to take care of all who wanted rooms."[3] Photo courtesy of the University of New Hampshire, Dimond Library, Isles of Shoals Collection.

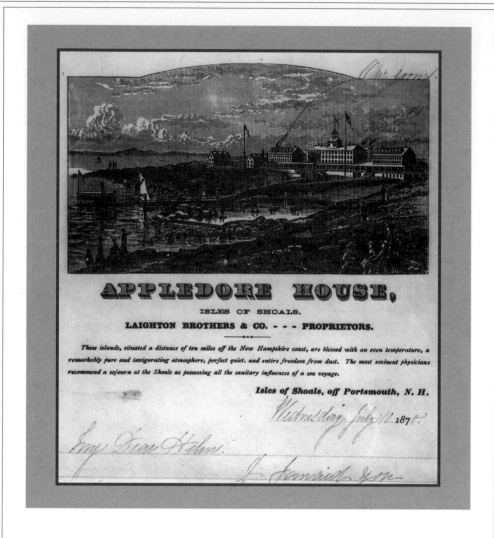

APPLEDORE HOUSE,
ISLES OF SHOALS.
LAIGHTON BROTHERS & CO. - - - PROPRIETORS.

These islands, situated a distance of ten miles off the New Hampshire coast, are blessed with an even temperature, a remarkably pure and invigorating atmosphere, perfect quiet, and entire freedom from dust. The most eminent physicians recommend a sojourn at the Shoals as possessing all the sanitary influences of a sea voyage.

Isles of Shoals, off Portsmouth, N. H.

Right: Photo of a piece of stationery from the Appledore House. Photo courtesy of the University of New Hampshire, Dimond Library, Isles of Shoals Collection.

because of Levi and Thomas, but in later years, they came to visit with the poet Celia.

Because the Appledore House was nearly self-sufficient, its operation involved a great deal of hard work for the Laighton Family. All the vegetables were raised on the island, and there were even sheep and cattle supplying mutton and beef. Thomas, Oscar, and Cedric did all the maintenance on the hotel, as well as the raising of the livestock and produce. Celia and her mother sewed linens and curtains all winter and cooked all summer. During the hotel season itself, Eliza was the chief cook and Celia the bottlewasher for the hoards of guests. At its peak, the hotel slept 500 guests and fed 900 at its tables. The hotel required a lot of Celia's physical strength and energy. Except for a few summers in the early years of her marriage, Celia spent every summer of her life out on the islands helping with the hotel.

APPLEDORE PUDDING

Butter a pudding dish and line it with stale cake; then fill it within three inches of the top with blueberries, blackberries, or currants. To one quart of blueberries or blackberries allow a half a cup of sugar; if currants allow one cupful. Cover the whole with cake, and wet with a half a tumbler of wine. Bake a half hour, and frost with the whites of two eggs; set back in the oven, and bake a light brown. To be eaten without sauce. [5]

RAISED DOUGHNUTS

One cup of sweet milk, one spoonful of butter, four of yeast, four of sugar, half a nutmeg, and flour to make a stiff batter; let this rise over night. In the morning roll out, cut in strips, with a jagging-iron, about four inches long and two inches wide, and fry. Common raised dough makes very nice ones to be eaten as soon as fried, either for breakfast or tea. Doughnuts should not be eaten before November or after April; indeed, they are not very healthful to eat at any time. Keep covered in a stone pot in the cellar. [6]

Left: "There is not one recipe in the book which has not been proved to be good. Many of the visitors to ...the Appledore House, Isles of Shoals, will find many dishes with which they expressed themselves pleased while the writer was pastry cook at those houses." Maria Parloa, The Appledore Cook Book Containing Practical Recipes for Plain and Rich Cooking, (Boston: Andrew F. Graves, 1880) P. 4.

Left: Dining Room of Appledore House. Photo courtesy of the University of New Hampshire, Dimond Library, Isles of Shoals Collection.

GRAHAM PIES

Into a pint of Graham flour, stir one teaspoonful of salt; wet with boiling water enough to make a stiff past. Roll this very thin, and cut into cakes about three inches in diameter; put into these a spoonful of applesauce and fold them. Bake on tin sheets. These can be eaten by any dyspeptic. [7]

ELIZA LAIGHTON'S FISH CHOWDER

Take either a cod or haddock, skin it, loosen the skin about the head, and draw it down towards the tail, when it will peel off easily. Then run your knife down the back close to the bone, which you take out. Cut your fish into small pieces, and wash in cold water. Put the head on to boil in about two quarts of water, and boil twenty minutes. Four pounds of fish, half cod and half haddock, if you can get two kinds, two onions, six potatoes, eight white browns, one quarter of pound salt pork, salt, pepper. Prepare the chowder as directed: Pare and slice potatoes thin. Place a layer of potatoes and onion in the pot, then a layer of fish, dredge in a little salt, pepper, and flour. Keep putting in alternate layers of potatoes and fish until all is used. Have ready a half a pound of salt pork fried brown. Pour this over the mixture. Split the crackers and lay on the top. Pour over the whole hot water enough to cover, and boil fifteen minutes, then wet two tablespoons of flour with one-third of a cup of cream. Stir this into the boiling chowder, let it boil up once, and serve. When you cannot get the white browns, pilot bread will answer. When a strong flavor of onions is desired, use four onions. [8]

Mrs. T. Laighton

Right: Guests would go off fishing and return with full loads of cod – some weighing over 40 pounds – and Eliza would use the fish for the guests' meals. One guest noted that the chowder alone was worth the price of a room! A collection of Eliza's recipes was published in The Appledore Cook Book *by Maria Parloa. Photo courtesy of the University of New Hampshire, Dimond Library, Isles of Shoals Collection.*

As with all inking, the fabric had to be prepared first. I ironed freezer paper onto the back of the fabric for stability. A spray of fabric finish was ironed into the front of the fabric to help prevent the ink from running.

Again, I always ink with a light touch! Strokes can always be made darker, but can never be made lighter! Go over letters with shading on the down strokes. The size of your writing is important. If you write too small, your shading will look like ink blots instead of letters. Always practice on scrap paper and then fabric before going to your final piece.

Fabric inking allowed me to handsomely celebrate the many guests who peopled the Appledore House – and Celia's life.

Ribbon roses and leaves were created to commemorate the vases of roses and other flowers that Celia made certain were always on the registration desk, to greet guests arriving at the Appledore House.

To make this block commemorating the Appledore House, I used a piece of the hotel's 1878 letterhead as a guide for the hotel register page, which is presented as a curled banner. I made a tracing of the page and penciled in all the names to determine proper placement before I inked them on fabric.

Guest Block

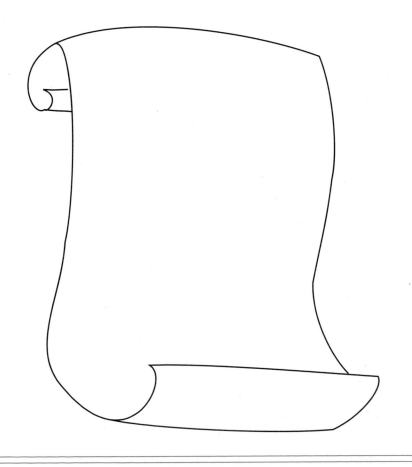

Vase of Roses

Instructions

FULL-BLOWN RIBBON ROSES

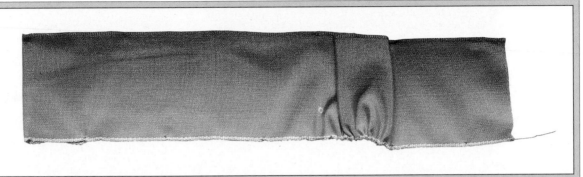

1 For a full blown rose, use 18 to 36 inches of wire-edged ribbon 1" to 2" wide. Begin to gather the ribbon by exposing about 1 inch of wire from each end of the ribbon. Be careful not to pull the wire. Gently push the ribbon toward the center of the wire.

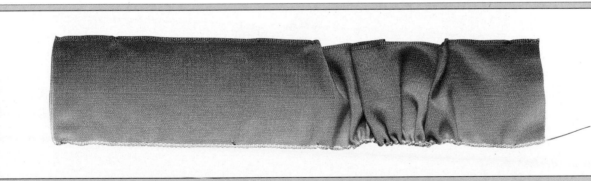

2 Work both edges alternately until the ribbon is gathered tightly, without forcing, on the wire.

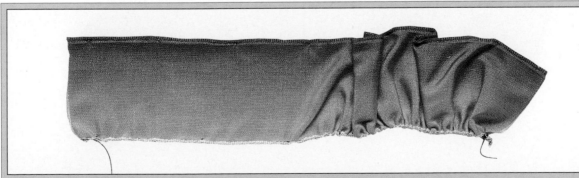

3 Secure the ribbon gathers from escaping by wrapping the wire around itself and the selvage edge.

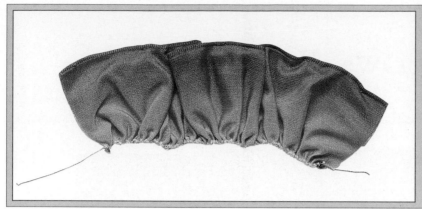

4 Secure or anchor the gathers on both ends of the gathered ribbon. Do not, as yet, cut off the excess wire.

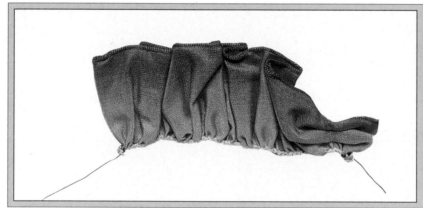

5 To form a center bud and stem handle, push the ungathered (top) edge of the ribbon down to the gathered (bottom) edge. Squeeze together.

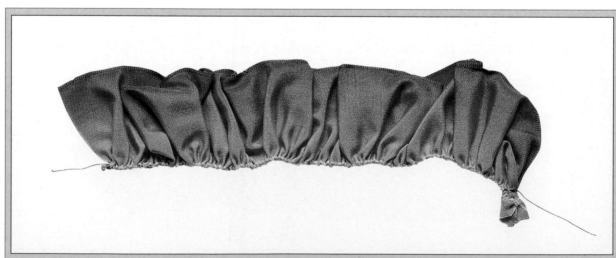

6 Wrap the excess wire around the squeezed ribbon to form a center bud and stem/handle.

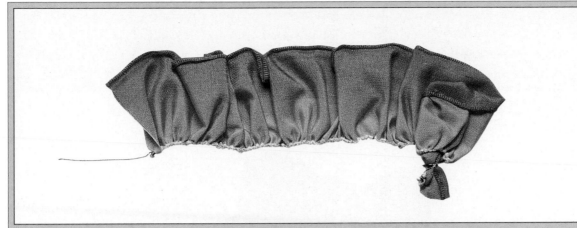

7 Begin to roll the stem/handle along the gathered ribbon bottom edge about two revolutions. At this point you may stitch the bottom rows together to prevent slippage.

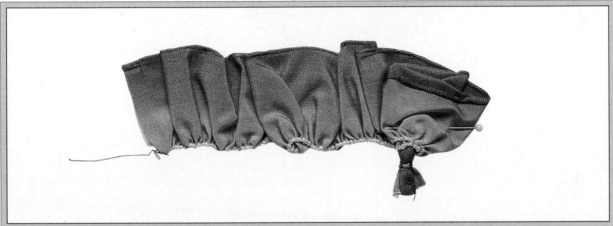

8 Now begin to spiral the gathered ribbon length up and away from the rose stem. The rose will now appear to grow or bloom!

9 Turn the rose upside down and secure each row to the previous row with a whipstitch. The rows should be approximately ⅛ to ¼ inches apart. The farther apart the rows, the larger your rose will "grow."

10 Fold the raw edge of the ribbon under, and stitch to the back of the rose. Realistic leaves may be cut from an accent fabric or ribbon leaves added. This rose is attached to the background with a few hidden stitches through the rose. Petals may be stitched into place with a couple of hidden stitches to achieve the desired look.

Rose variations: Roses may be made with any width of ribbon and any length from 18 to 36 inches. A rose just beginning to open may be made from a 9-inch length of ribbon.

RIBBON LEAVES

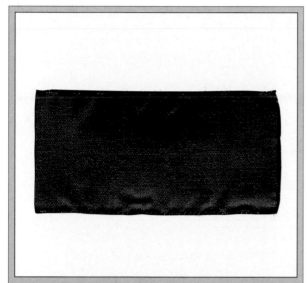

1 Use 3 inches of 1½ inch wide wire-edged green ribbon per single leaf.

3 Unfold the ribbon and fold stitched portion into a triangular shape.

2 Fold in half lengthwise. Using double thread, stitch a seam on one end. This step may be done on the sewing machine if you need lots of leaves in a hurry.

4 Turn triangular-folded end inside out and flatten. Wire will allow the triangular tip to hold its shape without further stitches.

5 Using double thread, stitch a row of running stitches on the remaining cut end.

6 Gather ribbon tightly and secure thread.

7 Repeat the above steps for multiple leaves.

This technique works with any width ribbon. Unwired ribbon can be used, but additional anchoring stitches will be needed to keep the leaf flat against the background fabric.

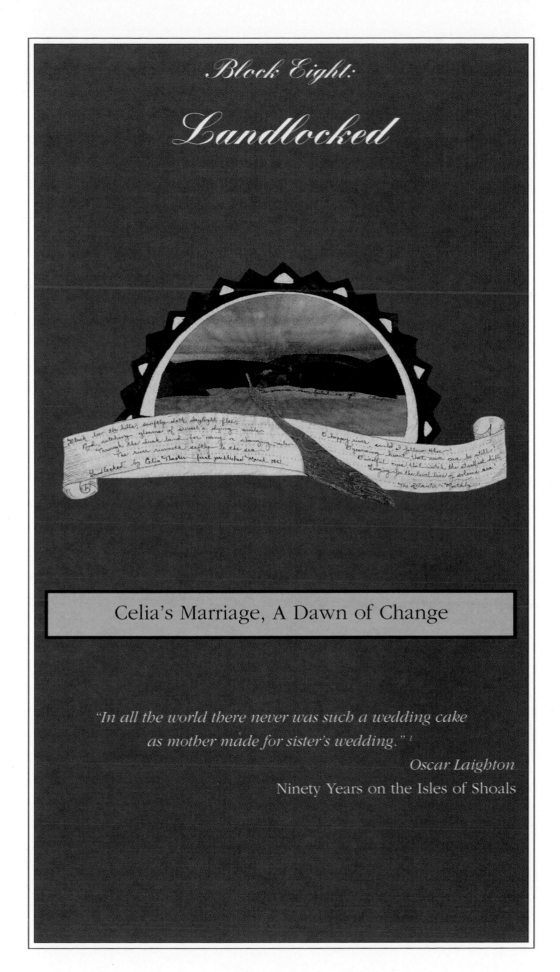

Block Eight:

Landlocked

Celia's Marriage, A Dawn of Change

*"In all the world there never was such a wedding cake
as mother made for sister's wedding."* [1]

Oscar Laighton
Ninety Years on the Isles of Shoals

Featured Flower:

Phlox.

Instructions

p. 89

Right: Photo of young Celia age 20, circa 1855. Photo courtesy of the University of New Hampshire, Dimond Library, Isles of Shoals Collection.

Far Right: Photo of Levi at the time of his marriage, 1851. Photo courtesy of Special Collections, Miller Library, Colby College, Waterville, ME.

On September 30, 1851, a beautiful fall day, Levi and Celia were married in the parlor of the Appledore House. Celia wore a dress of red merino wool made by her mother, and she carried a bouquet of pink sweet peas.

Oscar recalls this day, the parlor filled with scarlet huckleberry leaves, bright rose-haws, wild asters, beach goldenrod, and bright September sunshine: "Celia was married to Mr. Thaxter...before a distinguished gathering of friends and guests of the hotel....how magnificent the couple looked, standing up to be married before the dignified John Weiss." [2]

In a letter to his friend Higginson, Levi wrote: "We had a merry time, and then I took my dear wife home in the beautiful night, bright and clear with stars and a growing moon, and prayed God to strengthen me to make the hearth happy. I shall hope and try."[3] Levi and his new wife moved to his North Cottage to live, and life as Celia had known it was forever changed. Though only sixteen, she was now a wife, and within the year, would be a mother.

Soon, Levi took Celia to live in Massachusetts. How excited Celia must have been, going into a world of sights and experiences unknown to her on the island. Levi's family welcomed Celia, and she was to become lifelong friends with Levi's sister, Lucy Thaxter. Celia and Levi spent their first winter at the home of friends as Levi still did not have an occupation.

They returned to Appledore in 1852, as soon as the weather permitted, where they remained for the summer season. Celia was expecting their first child and wanted to be close to her mother. On the July 24, 1852, exactly six years from the day Levi had first arrived on the Isles of Shoals, a son was born to Celia and Levi. Karl Thaxter, the first child born on Appledore Island in almost one hundred years, was a special child. His difficult birth resulted in complications which would affect him for the rest of his life. He would be lame, and also would suffer from mental anxiety, depression, and violent attacks.

During the second summer of their married life, Levi accepted a temporary dual position on Star Island, as preacher and teacher for the fishermen's children. Levi and Celia lived in the island's old parsonage, and these were very happy times for them. Levi was a good teacher. They left Star Island in the

fall of 1854 and accepted the hospitality of their friends, the Curzons of Newburyport, Massachusetts. They moved into the Mill House on the banks of the Artichoke River, with their good friends living nearby. Their second son, John, was born there on November 29, 1854.

Life was difficult for this nineteen-year-old mother of two. Her husband was not the hard worker that her parents had been, and she was not allowed to bring in household help. Levi spent much time roaming the fields around his home, observing nature and collecting specimens for study. While at Harvard University, he became acquainted with Henry David Thoreau. Although Thoreau's disposition and personality did not lend themselves to close personal ties, he often

Left: Celia with John and Karl, 1856. Photo courtesy of the University of New Hampshire, Dimond Library, Isles of Shoals Collection.

Right: Levi with Roland, age 10, during a bird collecting expedition from Maine to Florida in 1868. Photo courtesy of Special Collections, Miller Library, Colby College, Waterville, ME.

took Levi and James Lowell on walks in open fields, pointing out many of nature's wonders. Levi continued these nature walks – some of them lasting months in various parts of the country – throughout his life.

Celia's third child, Roland, was born in 1858. By this time, Levi had all but given up trying to find a job. He became, instead, a gentleman of leisure. After living in friends' homes for five years, Levi and Celia moved into their own home when Levi's father purchased a "modest mansion" for them in Newtonville, Massachusetts, just north of Boston. Celia found herself caring for three small children and a huge ark of a house with no household help.

There was much work during these early years of marriage, but there were also moments of joy and peace. Each evening Levi read poetry to Celia by the fireside and played music on their piano. This relaxed her and inspired her to write her own verses. As their children grew older, though, these evenings by the fireside became less relaxing. It was up to Celia to find activities that would keep three young children quiet while Levi read poetry or played the piano. Knitting worked for a while. But the best idea was the making of a patchwork quilt.

Celia didn't enjoy sewing much because of all the sewing she did regularly for her family and the hotel, but the boys enjoyed it. They would painstakingly sew together the squares she cut. Each boy's work was quite identifiable – Karl's was dirty because he always had dirty hands, John's was puckery because

he was impatient, and Roland's was always nearly perfect! Celia later wrote a poem "Mozart at the Fireside" about these evenings by the fire.

Homesick for her family, Celia wrote many letters to them and always looked forward to receiving their letters. At first she wrote long separate letters to her entire family; then as time became less available, she simply wrote to her younger brother Cedric. Many of these letters were saved by his family and offer much insight into Celia's thoughts during those early years of marriage.

Celia would often send along with her letters the verses she composed in her head as she worked. One day a poem came to Celia as she was kneading bread in her Newtonville kitchen. She wrote it down

Left: Thaxter home on the Charles River in Newtonville, MA, just north of Boston. It still stands today, almost unchanged from over 150 years ago, on the corner of Nevada Street at 542 California Street. Photo courtesy of the University of New Hampshire, Dimond Library, Isles of Shoals Collection.

on a piece of grocery paper, all she had on hand at the moment. When she included the little poem in a letter to Cedric, he wrote back: "I am perfectly delighted with the little poem you so kindly sent me, and I shall keep it so long as I live, as a sad memorial of departed days as Bocky [Oscar] would say."[4]

Without Celia's knowledge, this poem was sent anonymously by a friend to James Russell Lowell, the editor of *The Atlantic Monthly*. Lowell read the poem, gave it the title "Landlocked," and published it in the March 18, 1861 issue. Celia could hardly believe her eyes when she read her poem for the first time in this popular magazine. It was one of the happiest moments in her life!

This first published poem was the central theme of my quilt block bearing the same name. The poem's first lines inspired the block's design: "Black lie the hills... swiftly daylight flees... the river runs to the sea." With a few sketches on paper, I was ready for fabric selection.

From my collection of hand-painted sky fabrics I chose a large piece that I thought would work for a sunset. I cut out a sky area window template from heavy paper. By sliding this window over the sky fabric, I was able to get just the view I wanted. I secured this area on the fabric by placing a freezer paper cutout of the sky over the window and ironing the template in place.

The hills quickly materialized, along with the green fields. For the river I selected a piece of blue marbleized fabric. I again used a window template on the marbleized fabric for the river. (A detailed explanation of this procedure is described in the Books and Letters block).

The banner was made by cutting a strip of paper long enough to fit under the block. Sample writing determined that the banner was too short to accommodate all the words, so a longer banner was cut. Shading turned the banner into a twisted scroll.

The wreath around the block is from Elly Sienkiewicz's Pattern 1 from *Baltimore Beauties and Beyond*, Volume II, C & T Publishing page 112, Hans Christian Andersen's Danish Hearts. I originally planned to use a wreath of flowers but then decided to use a paper-cut wreath, made with a dark floral print.

When I looked at the stitched wreath from afar, it resembled the sun's rays, so I inked a verse from another of Celia's poems under the black hills: "The sunrise never failed us yet!" The wreath and the poem represent the start of a new day in Celia's life. Golden sunrays quilted throughout the sky fall across the field.

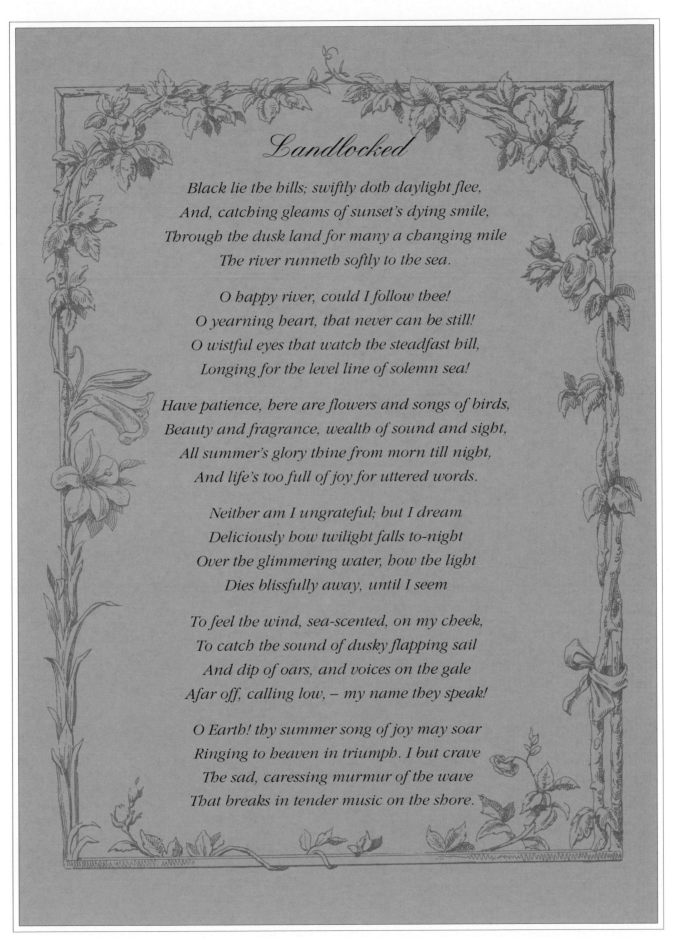

Landlocked

Black lie the hills; swiftly doth daylight flee,
And, catching gleams of sunset's dying smile,
Through the dusk land for many a changing mile
The river runneth softly to the sea.

O happy river, could I follow thee!
O yearning heart, that never can be still!
O wistful eyes that watch the steadfast hill,
Longing for the level line of solemn sea!

Have patience, here are flowers and songs of birds,
Beauty and fragrance, wealth of sound and sight,
All summer's glory thine from morn till night,
And life's too full of joy for uttered words.

Neither am I ungrateful; but I dream
Deliciously how twilight falls to-night
Over the glimmering water, how the light
Dies blissfully away, until I seem

To feel the wind, sea-scented, on my cheek,
To catch the sound of dusky flapping sail
And dip of oars, and voices on the gale
Afar off, calling low, – my name they speak!

O Earth! thy summer song of joy may soar
Ringing to heaven in triumph. I but crave
The sad, caressing murmur of the wave
That breaks in tender music on the shore.

Landlocked Block

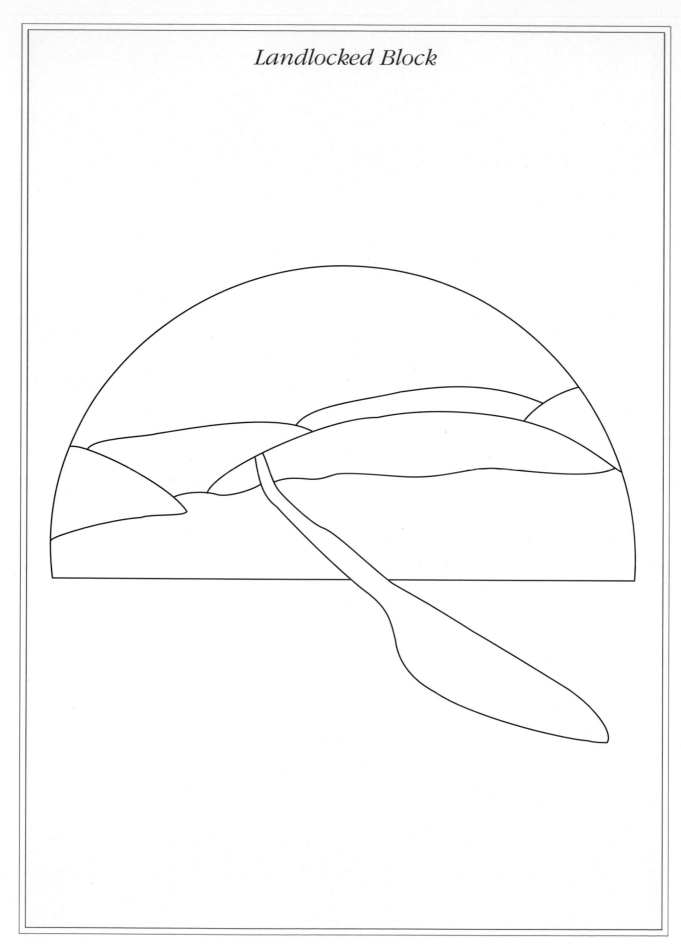

PHLOX

Phlox symbolize proposals of love and sweet dreams. To ease the pain of homesickness for her island family, Celia transplanted some perennial flowers from her mother's garden to her landlocked home, as a pleasant reminder of happy times and places.

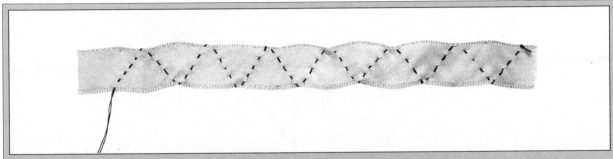

1 Use a 6½ inch portion of ¾ inch wide soft satin unwired ribbon per flower. Use matching thread, about 36 inches in length, doubled and knotted. Triangles will be stitched in the ribbon at one inch intervals using tiny running stitches. When you reach the selvage edge the thread will lie over the selvage. The triangles are one inch wide at their base.

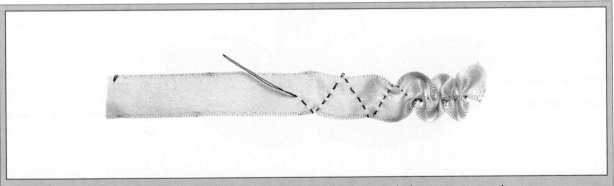

2 Pull the thread gently after stitching 2 or 3 triangles. Each triangle becomes a petal.

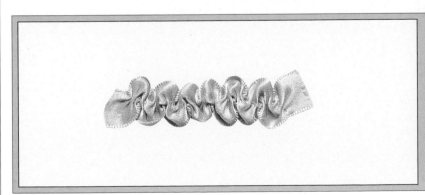

3 Continue stitching triangles and gathering until you have 6 complete petals on each side. Do not pull very tightly. Do not anchor off the thread until you have completed Step 4.

4 Bring the cut edges together to form a petaled circle. Petals may have to be readjusted, either tightened or loosened, to form a flat circle. If the petals were gathered too tightly, you may have to loosen them up a bit in order to form a petaled circle that will lie flat. When you are satisfied with the flower's appearance, anchor off with a couple of overlapping stitches and cut the thread.

5 Attach to background fabric with stitches through the gathered sections of the flower. Center petals may be anchored to a central point for a controlled center (see above) or left "free."

Block Nine:
The Island Cottage

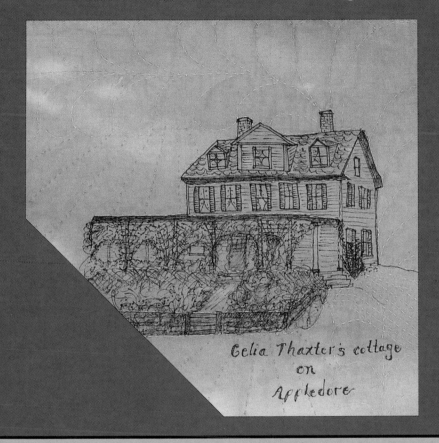

Celia Thaxter's cottage on Appledore

Years of Conflict: Daughter, Mother, Wife, Author

"I'm afraid I never put my heart into anything that doesn't belong to the sea." [1]

Celia Thaxter
Letters of Celia Thaxter

Featured Flowers:

Morning-glories

and Buds

Instructions

p. 96 & 99

Wisteria,

Instructions

p. 101

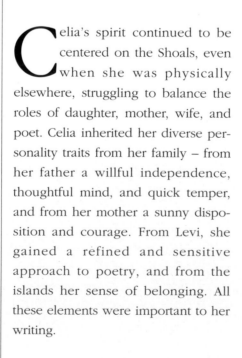

Right: A formal portrait of Celia Thaxter as an established poet, circa 1880. Photo courtesy of the University of New Hampshire, Dimond Library, Isles of Shoals Collection.

Celia's spirit continued to be centered on the Shoals, even when she was physically elsewhere, struggling to balance the roles of daughter, mother, wife, and poet. Celia inherited her diverse personality traits from her family – from her father a willful independence, thoughtful mind, and quick temper, and from her mother a sunny disposition and courage. From Levi, she gained a refined and sensitive approach to poetry, and from the islands her sense of belonging. All these elements were important to her writing.

The early years of Celia's marriage were happy years. In an 1857 letter she writes, "Such good evenings as we have! And they are so fascinating sometimes we don't break up the meeting till past eleven, never till after ten. We draw the table up to the roaring fire, and I take my work, and Levi reads to me...." [2]

Unfortunately, this happy scene was to change. As it became apparent that Karl had developmental problems, Levi withdrew from most of his family and spent his time with his second son, John. When Roland was born in 1858, Levi became very attentive to this third-born son, practically raising him by himself.

Celia began to be left alone much of the time, as Levi spent more time with male college friends and his two younger sons. Celia found solace in the many letters she wrote to her female friends. The stress of these situations and Levi's lack of attention and financial support took their toll on the marriage. Financial stress, though, lessened with the publication of her poem "Landlocked" in *The Atlantic Monthly*.

Though the poem was published without the author's name, as was the custom, Celia was an instant success! Other magazines wanted Celia's verses. With fireside poetry the rage in America, Celia found that she could make money from the publication of her poems and submitted several each month to various publications, receiving $10 a piece. Her economic success allowed her to hire help for chores and purchase a sewing machine for making shirts and patching trousers. With the publication of her poems, Celia had financial security for the first time in her married life. She continued to write poems ("for a kitchen stove" or "a carpet" [3]) whenever she found a moment amid her household chores.

Her reputation was so prominent that when Emily Dickinson's editor, Thomas Wentworth Higginson, submitted the first edition of her poems to Houghton Mifflin, he was rejected because they "already had a female poet – Celia Thaxter." [4] The many demands on Celia's time forced her to write most of her poetry in a state of physical, mental, and emotional exhaustion.

Levi must have been proud of Celia's accomplishments. He had been her tutor, and introduced her to the contemporary poets whose works inspired her. But he would never comment on Celia's poetry, though she longed for recognition from him. Life became more difficult for Celia and Levi.

As Celia became more successful, Levi and Celia's lives drifted further apart. Celia spent her summers on Appledore helping her family with the running of the hotel. Sometimes Levi and the boys would join Karl and her there, staying in Levi's North Cottage, enjoying the enchantment of the islands.

During one such visit Levi and Oscar were returning from Portsmouth with supplies when a sudden summer storm overtook them. Celia watched their boat being tossed about, unsure whether her husband or brother would survive. Her poem "All's Well" captures the young mother's desperation as she helplessly watched from the shore. Both survived, but the lives of Levi and Celia would never be the same.

That afternoon Levi vowed to never again set foot on the Shoals. He sold his share of the island and his cottage to Thomas Laighton and left for good. This event further drove them apart, for Celia was continually called back to the island to help with the hotel and with her aging parents. As Thomas's health deteriorated, his illness often required her to hurry to the Shoals at

Right: Thomas and Eliza's cottage which became Celia's after their death. Photo courtesy of the University of New Hampshire, Dimond Library, Isles of Shoals Collection.

a moment's notice.

The hotel was thriving, but the commotion of 500 guests was too much for the aging Thomas and Eliza Laighton. Oscar and Cedric built a cottage for their parents near the hotel, so they could have some privacy. Thomas B. Laighton died on May 16, 1866, and was laid to rest on the top of the little hill where Cedric had first found violets. This was the first burial on Appledore in over one hundred years. Thomas had realized his dream of making the Shoals famous again, but he died not knowing the important role his daughter Celia would have in the "making of the Shoals."

Levi began to leave Celia alone more frequently as he went on nature expeditions, often taking with him his sons John and Roland, who both developed a love of nature. John would eventually become a gentleman farmer and Roland a dis-

tinguished professor of botany at Harvard University. Celia could not be a part of these trips, because Karl was not welcome.

In 1869 Levi suffered the first of many attacks of an illness from which he never recovered. His health required that he spend winters in a warmer climate. So he began spending winters in Florida with his two younger sons, while Celia and Karl were on the Island with her mother and brothers. Eliza's health was failing, and Celia was needed almost constantly at her side.

Eliza's health continued to deteriorate and in fall 1877 the decision was made to move her to Portsmouth. The winters were harsh on the island, and Eliza would be more comfortable in Portsmouth with a doctor close by. After 38 years, Eliza had returned to the city.

Eliza's last words were to her sons, Oscar and Cedric: "Be good to

Sister! She has had a hard life."[5] After Eliza died on November 14, 1877, Celia and her brothers buried her on Appledore on the hill where the violets grew, next to her devoted husband, Thomas. Celia brought flowers from Portsmouth for her Mother's burial – not pale flowers, but the brightest flowers she could find. Devastated by Eliza's death, Celia wrote many poems in her memory and even attended seances hoping to make contact with her.

That spring Celia moved back to Eliza's cottage on Appledore. She continued to tend Eliza's beautiful garden and made it her own. At times she didn't know how she would get through another day. One of the guests at the hotel, William Mason, a pianist, visited Celia in her parlor and played music all day, all summer long. Somehow the beauti-ful sounds brought Celia out of the depths of her despair, and into the world of the living.

After her parents' deaths, their cottage became Celia's and was known as the Thaxter Cottage. Celia began inviting talented guests for afternoons of music, poetry, and conversation.

It seemed natural that a sketch of Celia's cottage should be included in the quilt. Working from a photograph, I enlarged, traced, and inked the cottage as I did images inked on earlier blocks. Fortunately, you don't need to be an artist to create such blocks; you only need to be able to trace.

In the front yard of this cottage lay Celia's famous garden.

Instructions follow for the morning-glory and wisteria vines that shaded the piazza of Celia's cottage.

Left: Celia with her mother in Eliza's parlor on Appledore. Photo courtesy of the University of New Hampshire, Dimond Library, Isles of Shoals Collection.

Instructions

MORNING-GLORIES

M orning-glories symbolize the loveliness of life.

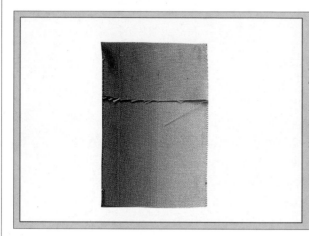

1 Cut a 12 inch piece of 1½ inch wide ombré (shaded) blue wire-edged ribbon. Decide which shading the parts of your morning-glory should be. The flower's center color will be the right edge of the ribbon and the actual color of the finished flower will the left side of the ribbon. Fold the ribbon over ¾ inch in length.

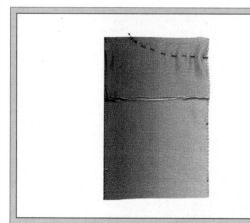

2 Using a single matching thread, stitch an overlapping stitch over both selvages – right side edge ¼ inch down from the fold. This forms the anchoring point for your seam line. Stitch a diagonal seam line, 1 inch long, beginning at anchoring point at the selvage edge and ending ¼" away from the left edge. Be sure stitches are tiny. End with 2 or 3 overlapping stitches. Trim thread close.

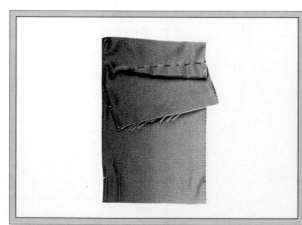

3 Fold this stitched dart forward (toward you) and refold the ribbon ¼ inch away from the stitched dart.

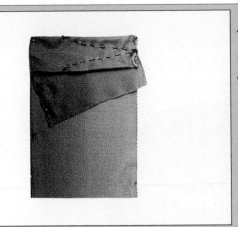

4 Begin to stitch the second dart in the same place where the first dart was started. There will be no ribbon gap between the darts. Continue to stitch the dart in the same manner as in Step 2.

5 Continue to fold sewn darts toward you and refold ribbon ¼ inch beyond for the next dart. Complete sewing darts until a circle is formed. Just how many darts are sewn is up to you. The more darts you sew, the flatter the flower will be. Sew fewer darts for an open trumpet-shaped flower.

6 Fold cut edges together and stitch a narrow seam to close the flower darts and flower center.

7 Use several lengths of golden yellow embroidery floss to form a knotted center. Insert into the center of the morning-glory. Secure with needle and thread, pulling the center opening closed with a couple of stitches.

MORNING-GLORY BUDS

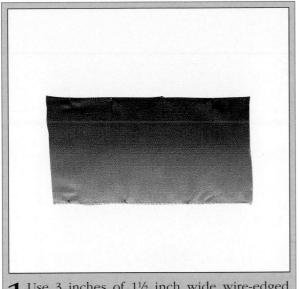

1 Use 3 inches of 1½ inch wide wire-edged ribbon per bud.

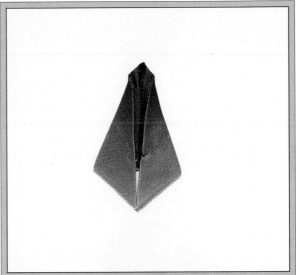

3 Fold left and right folded edges into center.

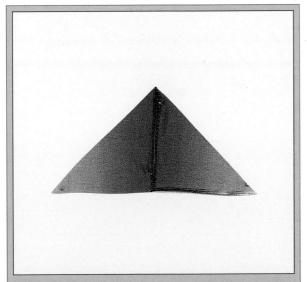

2 Fold in half and crease wire for center guide line. Fold the top selvage edges in to center crease. Ribbon will resemble a tent at this step.

4 Pin to hold folds together.

5 Remove the pin and hold the base of the bud with one hand while tightly twisting ribbon with second hand. Secure base with anchoring stitches. Trim the uneven edges of ribbon ¼ inch beyond the anchoring stitches. The wire will keep the bud twisted.

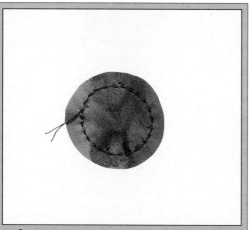

6 Bud case. Draw a 1 inch circle on green fabric. Use a double thread and stitch tiny running stitches on the pencil line. Cut ¼ inch beyond stitching.

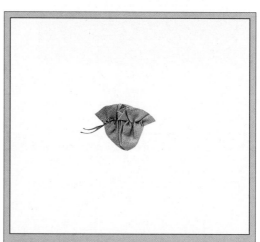

7 Pull the thread and gather the circle into a cap or yo-yo.

8 Insert the morning-glory bud into the opening and continue gathering tightly. Secure with anchoring stitches. Attach the bud to a morning-glory stem with a couple of hidden stitches through the cap.

Instructions

WISTERIA

Wisteria symbolize a daughter's sweetness and such sentiments as "welcome, fair stranger and I cling to thee."

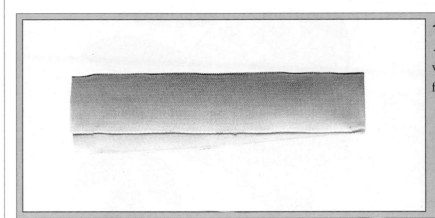

1 Use a 36-inch portion of a 1 inch wide ombré (purple to white) wire-edged ribbon per flower.

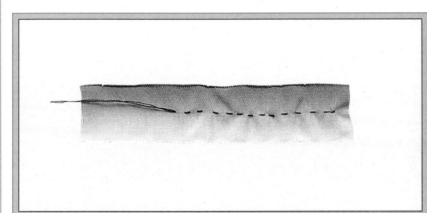

2 Using thread of a matching color (36 inches in length, doubled and knotted), stitch a row of running stitches through the center length of the ribbon.

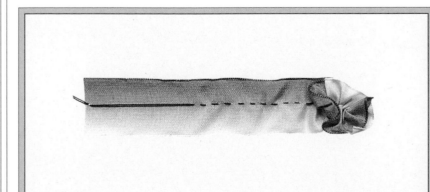

3 Gently gather the ribbon every few inches. Do not pull too tightly. Ribbon should swirl about itself as it is pulled.

BLOCK NINE **101**

4 Stop when you have stitched and gathered the entire yard of ribbon, leaving the needle and thread attached. Mold the ribbon into a triangular shape. When shape is pleasing and no gaps are visible, secure the ribbon to itself with hidden stitches. The flower is attached to the background fabric through the gathered sections with hidden stitches.

Block Ten:

Books and Letters

Celia's Parlor

""*What heavenly music has resounded from those walls,
what mornings and evenings of pleasantness
have flown by in that room!* " [1]

Celia Thaxter
An Island Garden

Featured Flower:

Soft Fabric Rose,

Instructions

p. 113

In the 1870's, Boston was the peak of America's intellectual and literary blooming, and Celia's success quickly earned her a place in its literary society. In the summer, her friends followed her to the Shoals, where she invited to her cottage parlor authors, artists, and musicians who had come to the islands for rest and inspiration. The atmosphere was very stimulating, the music heavenly, and the flowers colorful and aromatic. Her parlor became a salon in the true sense of the word and served as a model for American summer art colonies.

Celia became acquainted with Boston's literary and cultural society through James T. Fields, her editor/publisher at *The Atlantic Monthly*. Fields and his young wife Annie took Celia under their wing and became her most intimate friends and counselors. She was devoted to them and they had a tremendous influence on her, both socially and professionally. Annie became Celia's confidant, as the poet poured out her heart in letters written over the years.

Left: Flower arrangements on altar and shrine in Celia's parlor. Photo courtesy of the University of New Hampshire, Dimond Library, Isles of Shoals Collection.

Left: Another view of Celia's parlor featuring the window seat in Celia's favorite corner where she spent many relaxing afternoons gazing at the small table beside her that held the choicest blooms of the day. The corner was immortalized in Childe Hassam's painting Room of Flowers. Photo courtesy of the University of New Hampshire, Dimond Library, Isles of Shoals Collection.

I had originally planned to have my block about this important part of Celia's life represent Celia's parlor with all its Victorian complexity. My journal notes and early thoughts describe a pen sketch of the parlor with walls of paintings and photographs as the background. The foreground would have vases of flowers. The background fabric would have to be green, as Celia's walls were painted in her favorite restful color.

However, this block eventually became quite simple in design. Books, letters, and china painting were the focus of Celia's life in her later years. Once I decided on those elements, the block quickly began to design itself.

On a desk, in her parlor, would be significant books in Celia's life and letters she sent and received. The two letters in the block are addressed to Celia Thaxter, Appledore Island, Maine, with a stamp and postmark from Boston, Massachusetts. These inked details may go unnoticed by the viewer of the quilt, but I enjoyed researching and adding them.

The wreath surrounding this block was inspired by Pattern 46, *Baltimore Beauties and Beyond, Volume I – Pattern Companion*, C & T Publishing, Elly Sienkiewicz, p. 128, The Album Wreath. I based my choice of flowers on the symbolic language of flowers. Beginning with the upper left side of the wreath: white clover symbolizes "Think of me." A four-leaf clover was found pressed in a book of Celia's letters

that I had purchased, so I used it as it symbolizes good luck, good education, hard work, and industry. The forget-me-nots symbolize remembrance; true love, forget me not. The golden zinnia, fringed and ruched, symbolizes thoughts of absent friends. The ribbon rose symbolizes love. The bow out of Baltimore blue ties past to present. The pansy is cut whole cloth and symbolizes "You occupy my thoughts." Yellow acacia represents friendship or platonic love. Oak geranium leaves represent true friendship.

The leaves are a combination of realistic leaves cut whole-cloth from fabric and solid fabric leaves with inked veins. Several gold-plated leaf buttons are added for sunshine accents.

The background of the block is quilted with golden sunrays streaming through a window to brighten the room. Celia's books, letters to friends, and family and flowers brightened her life.

Books and Letters

Left: Vase of Roses, detail from the right border of the quilt, *A TRIBUTE TO CELIA THAXTER.* Photo Richard Walker.

"Near my own seat in a sofa corner at one of the south windows stands yet another small table, covered with a snow-white linen cloth embroidered in silk as white and lustrous as silver. On this are gathered every day all the rarest and loveliest flowers as they blossom, that I may touch them, dwell upon them, breathe their delightful fragrance and adore them. Here are kept the daintiest and most delicate of the vases which may best set off the flowers' loveliness, – the smallest of the collection, for the table is only large enough to hold a few."[8]

SOFT FABRIC ROSE

1 This rose is made with a 2½ inch-wide strip of fabric, cut either on the straight or on the bias of the fabric's grain. Any fabric may be used, but a silk-like fabric makes a very soft and elegant rose. Cut the strip at least 24 to 45 inches wide. Strips may be pieced together if the fabric is not long enough.

2 Fold in half length-wise and iron press fold. This fold will become the top or outside edge of the rose.

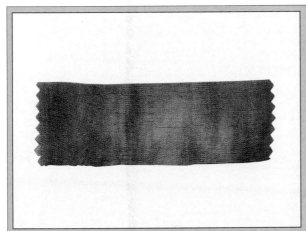

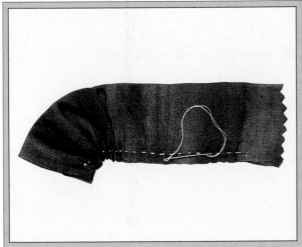

3 Use 36 inches of matching thread, doubled and knotted. Stitch both bottom cut edges together with a row of running stitches. Stop the stitches and gather the fabric every few inches along the way. Do not wait until you have stitched the entire strip. You might make the rose too big. Gently roll the gathered strip around itself, "jelly roll" fashion, keeping the cut bottom edges together, until the rose is the size you prefer. When you have reach that size, secure the gathers with a couple of overlapping stitches and cut the thread. Cut off the excess, unstitched fabric and save for another rose.

4 Fold the right cut edge over towards you to form a center bud and a stem/handle. Secure with a pin. Begin to roll the center around itself, taking care to keep the bottom cut edges even. Stitch the cut edges to each other with overcast or overlapping stitches. Fold the end strip down and attach to the back side of the rose.

5 Rose petals may be adjusted to your liking and secured with hidden stitches. The rose is attached to the background fabric with hidden stitches throughout the petals.

Block Eleven:

View through the Garden Gate

Celia's Garden

"This is what I enjoy! To wear my old clothes every day, grub in the ground, dig dandelions, and eat them too, plant my seeds and watch them...."[1]

Celia Thaxter
Heavenly Guest

Featured Flowers:

Sunflowers,

Instructions

p. 125

Foxgloves,

Instructions

p. 129

With fewer responsibilities after the death of her mother, Celia was able to spend many delightful days in her island garden with her flowers. When she was in her garden all her cares disappeared, and her flowers were her only concern. She nurtured them. She studied them with a scientist's scrutiny. She loved them! And they responded, blooming beautifully as they did for no other.

She says of her flower garden, "I feel the personality of each flower, and I find myself greeting them as if they were human...They stand in their peace and purity and lift themselves to my adoring gaze as if they knew my worship, – so calm, so sweet, so delicate radiant, I lose myself in the tranquility of their happiness."[2]

I know much of Celia's beloved garden because of the wonderful descriptions in her last book *An Island Garden*, which chronicles a year's cycle of growth. This classic in gardening literature was written during the last winter of Celia's life, at the urging of her many friends. Childe Hassam's impressionistic paintings are included in the volume, helping us visualize Celia's descriptions.

Celia's was an old-fashioned garden, similar to one her grandmother might have planted, with flowers in a casual arrangement: tall ones against the fence and shorter ones toward the front. She planted the flowers for their color, their fragrance, and textures; and poppies, sweet peas, and roses were among her favorites.

Celia's garden was also a friendship garden. She planted seeds and cuttings sent to her from all over the country. She also gave cuttings of

Right: The garden and lush, shady, vine-covered cottage in its prime at the end of summer, from a photograph by Karl Thaxter. Photo courtesy of the University of New Hampshire, Dimond Library, Isles of Shoals Collection.

Left: Walking up the front path to Celia's cottage. (1905) "Like the musician, the painters, the poet, and the rest, the true lover of flowers is born, not made." [3] *Photo courtesy of the University of New Hampshire, Dimond Library, Isles of Shoals Collection.*

Left: Inspirational photograph for the garden gate block on the quilt. From an original photograph by Karl Thaxter. *Photo courtesy of the University of New Hampshire, Dimond Library, Isles of Shoals Collection.*

her own plants to friends. Her garden was famous even in its own time. Many people came to the island especially to view it. One visitor relates her disappointment: "A great part of the beauty of Mrs. Thaxter's house in the Isles of Shoals was made up of flowers. It was far more enjoyable than her garden, where the flowers grew luxuriantly at their own sweet wills, or at the will of the planter, never troubling their heads about agreeing with their neighbors. I remember it as a disappointment that a woman with so exquisite a sense of combination and graduation in the arrangement of flowers, should have so little thought of color effect in her garden." [4]

However, Celia's garden was a picking garden. The flowers merely grew in the garden, their moment of glory came when they were in

Celia's hand. Celia used her garden for her artistic endeavors: flower arranging, china painting, and painting watercolor illustrations for books of poetry.

Celia often awoke at dawn and soon was out with her flowers, tending them with such love that they had no choice but to bloom beautifully. She loved the process of gardening, to feel the earth in her hands, to marvel at the miracle of a seed sprouting into a beautiful creation. Even the tools she used were sacred in her hands.

She hated the enemies of her garden with a similar passion and attacked them with a vengeance. For insects she had a myriad of bottles and tins filled with chemicals and powders. She was constantly protecting her newly planted gardens from the many of birds that descended on

Right: Early summer view of the chicken wire framework attached to the piazza. Celia planted morning-glories, nasturtiums, wild cucumbers, hops…anything that would climb, to provide shade for her sunny piazza. Photo courtesy of the University of New Hampshire, Dimond Library, Isles of Shoals Collection.

Right: Celia's parlor with flower arrangements and artwork for the pleasure of her guests...feasts for the eyes. Photo courtesy of the University of New Hampshire, Dimond Library, Isles of Shoals Collection.

Left: Detail from the lower left border of the quilt, A TRIBUTE TO CELIA THAXTER. Photo: Richard Walker.

the island during their spring migration, in search of any newly planted seed or seedlings. It was a constant battle to keep safe what had been sown.

Celia's toughest enemy was the slug, which she battled for some time to no avail. She comments: "In the thickest of my fight with the slugs someone said to me, 'Everything living has its enemy; the enemy of the slug is the toad. Why don't you import toads?' I snatched at the hope held out to me, and immediately wrote to a friend...."[5] Soon Celia received a box from Portsmouth, New Hampshire, filled with earth and 90 toads, which Celia soon let loose to eat the slugs. To this day there are no slugs on the island.

Hummingbirds came to the island in August. They were usually timid and would quickly dart away if disturbed by anything or anyone, except for one hummingbird. He lived on a dry twig among the larkspur and was quite tame. He hovered over Celia as she worked among her flowers.

Then one day in August there was a terrible storm on the Island, after which Celia went into her garden to remedy any damage. Busy righting plants, she came upon her precious pet hummingbird. Its tiny claws clung to the stem of a poppy-seed pod, as if it were holding on for dear life. Its eyes were shut and its body was cold. Celia cradled its frozen body in the palm of her hand

Right: "In the name of the Prophet, Toad!" Detail from the quilt, A TRIBUTE TO CELIA THAXTER. Inked drawing by Andrew Labanaris. Photo: Richard Walker.

Left: Detail from the border of the quilt, *A TRIBUTE TO CELIA THAXTER*. *"He is so tame he never stirs from his twig for anybody, no matter how near a person may come; he alights on my arms and hands and hair unafraid; he rifles the flowers I hold, when I am gathering them, and I sometimes think he is the very most charming thing in the garden."* [6] *Photo: Richard Walker.*

and breathed upon him for nearly half an hour. Finally, she felt a pulse. She placed him in little basket of fluff with a small vial of sugar water, putting this cradle among the sunflowers. Soon the warmth of the sun had revived him. He opened his eyes and was soon "diving deep into each winged blossom for his breakfast of honey."[7]

Celia's garden and all its inhabitants delighted and inspired her to write many poems. As we read these poems today, we can almost smell the flowers and feel the golden sunshine on our shoulders.

The inspiration for the garden gate block came from a black and white photograph of Celia's garden taken by her son Karl, who developed an interest in photography. I liked the angle, looking through and beyond the garden gate.

This block was the most difficult to execute in fabric, with many miniature dimensional fabrics and ribboned flowers filling the garden plot. I kept adding more and more flowers until I felt I had achieved the sort of abundance of flowering blooms that was found in Celia's garden. Embroidery, buttons, and beaded accents completed the blooms. A brown marbleized fabric provided a touch of realism to the fence and garden path.

My Garden

It blossomed by the summer sea,
A tiny space of tangled bloom
Wherein so many flowers found room,
A miracle it seemed to be!

Up from the ground, alert and bright,
The pansies laughed in gold and jet,
Purple and pied, and mignonette
Breathed like a spirit of delight.

Flaming the rich nasturtiums ran
Along the fence, and marigolds
"Opened afresh their starry folds"
In beauty as the day began,

While ranks of scarlet poppies gay
Waved when the soft south-wind did blow,
Superb in sunshine, to and fro,
Like soldiers proud in brave array.

And tall blue larkspur waved its spikes
Against the sea's deep violet,
That every breeze makes deeper yet
With splendid azure where it strikes;

And rosy-pale sweet-peas climbed up,
And phloxes spread their colors fine,
Pink, white, and purple, red as wine,
And fire burned in the escholtzia's cup.

More dear to me than words can tell
Was every cup and spray and leaf,
Too perfect for a life so brief
Seemed every star and bud and bell.

And many a maiden, fairer yet,
Came smiling to my garden gay,

Whose graceful head I decked always
With pansy and with mignonette.

Such slender shapes of girlhood young
Haunted that little blooming space,
Each with a more delightful face
Than any flower that ever sprung!

O shadowy shapes of youthful bloom!
How fair the sweet procession glides
Down memory's swift and silent tides,
Till lost in doubtful mists of gloom!

Year after year new flowers unfold,
Year after year fresh maidens fair,
Scenting their perfume on the air,
Follow and find their red and gold.

And while for them the poppies blaze
I gather, brightening into mine
The eyes of vanished beauty shine,
That gladdened long-lost summer days.

Where are they all who wide have ranged?
Where are the flowers of other years?
What ear the wistful question hears?
Ah, some are dead and all are changed.

And still the constant earth renews
Her treasured splendor, still unfold
Petals of purple and of gold
Beneath the sunshine and the dews.

But for her human children dear
Whom she has folded to her breast,
No beauty wakes them from their rest,
Nor change they with the changing year. [8]

Garden Gate

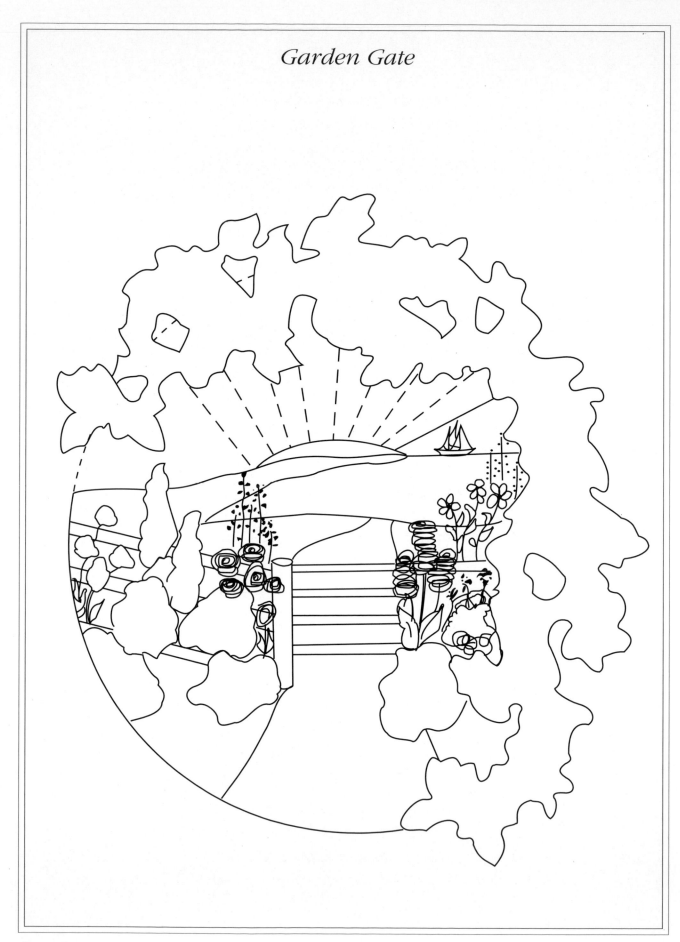

SUNFLOWERS

Sunflowers symbolize loyalty, adoration, and haughtiness. These sunflowers and the foxgloves that follow figured very prominently in Celia's garden. Although they are represented in miniature in the Garden Gate Block, they are seen in all their glory on the quilt's right border.

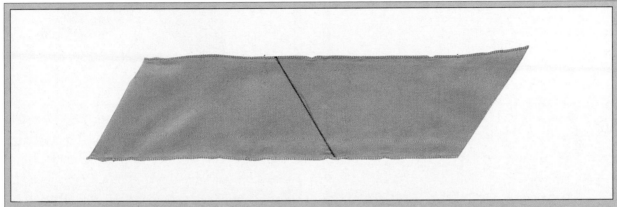

1 19 inches of 1½ inch wide ribbon will make 6 sunflower petals for a single-rayed sunflower, if the petals are cut as indicated above. For a double rayed sunflower, use an additional 19 inches of ribbon. Make a template from Step 2, and mark petals on ribbon with pencil.

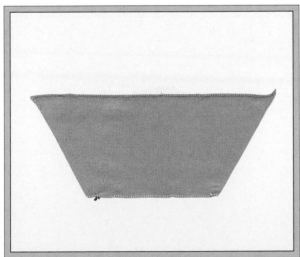

2 Cut petal sections and position each ribbon petal, so that the narrow selvage section is the bottom edge and widest selvage section is the top edge.

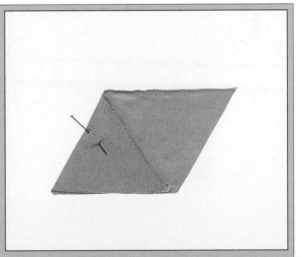

3 Fold the left cut edge toward the right side to lie even with the bottom selvage edge. Pin the left folded edge.

Reprinted by permission of C & T Publishing. Originally published in Elly Sienkiewicz's
Dimensional Appliqué: Baskets, Blooms & Baltimore Borders.

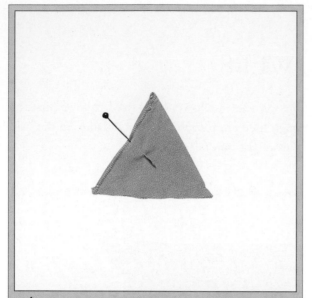

4 Repeat with right cut edge. Top selvage will lie on top of first fold. Pin together. Repeat with the other five cut petals.

6 Pick up the next petal and stitch as you did in the previous step. You will be stitching petals one after another, keeping them all connected on the same thread. When you have all 6 petals completed, connect together to form a circle, with a couple of overlapping stitches. If you would like a double-rayed sunflower, repeat Steps 1 to 6.

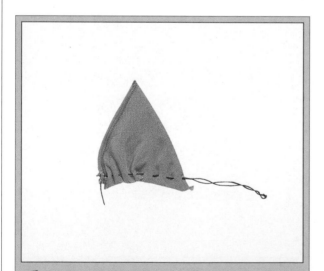

5 Using matching thread (36 inches in length, doubled and knotted), stitch a row of running stitches along the wide bottom edges. Gather as tightly as possible and anchor off thread, but do not cut thread.

7 For the center disk, cut a 1½ inch circle from dark brown fabric. A solid, print, paisley, metallic, cotton, velvet, or corduroy may be used. Stitch a row of running stitches just inside the cut edge.

8 Gently gather to form a small yo-yo type of gathered center. For a more dimensional look, add some stuffing to the center of the yo-yo.

9 Stitch the finished yo-yo to the center area of the sunflower petals. Beads may be added as an extra touch to the center disk.

10 To make a large sunflower, use 1½ yards of ribbon to make 15 petals and keep them together in a string or connected unit. Cut a 2½ inch circle of batting and a 3½ inch circle of brown fabric for the center disk. Baste the fabric over the circle of batting. Form a circle of petals and appliqué the center disk to cover the raw edges of the petals. Beads may be added to the center as an optional bit of sparkle.

Note: If you are making a double-rayed sunflower, position the two sunflower sections on top of each other, so that their petals alternate. Stitch the two layers together through their center edges. Then add stuffing and a center disk.

FOXGLOVES

Foxgloves symbolize: "I am not ambitious for myself, but for you." Foxgloves are clustered flowers constructed from individually fashioned "quarter" roses (so named because they use a quarter yard of ribbon each). A full foxglove flower may include as many as 6 to 8 separate florets.

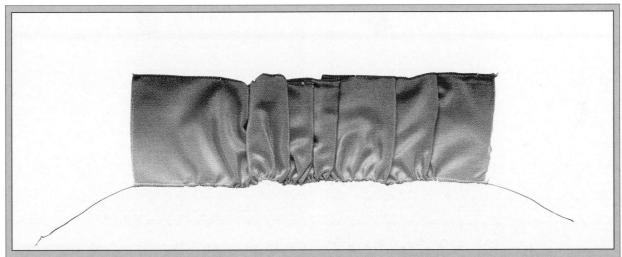

1 For each floret, 9 inches of 1½ inch wire-edged ribbon are needed. On one end of the ribbon, expose about 1 inch of wire from each edge. Be careful not to pull the wire out too quickly. Gently gather the ribbon along the wire as tightly as it will go without forcing.

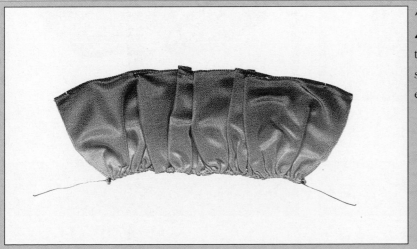

2 Secure the ribbon gathers from escaping by wrapping the wire around itself and the selvage edge. Do this on both ends.

3 Form a center bud and stem by folding back (away from you) the top ¼ inch of ribbon. Fold the right edge over (toward you) at a right angle. Refer to the diagram below to understand this step using ungathered ribbon. Squeeze the stem end and wrap with wire. Excess wire can be clipped off at this point.

4 Begin to roll or twirl the stem/handle.

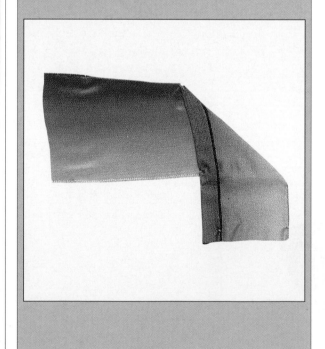

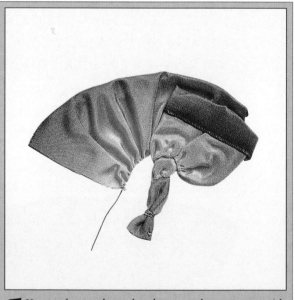

5 Keep the gathered selvage edges even with the first full revolution.

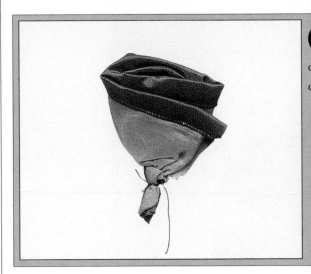

6 Continue to twirl or roll the stem, bringing the next rows down the stem. This will result in the center portion being a little higher than the next layer of petals.

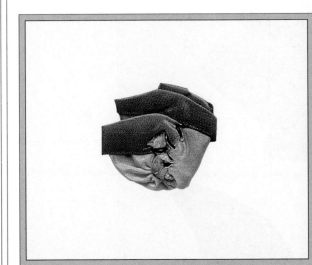

7 Fold raw ending edge to the back and secure to the flower with a few stitches. Turn the stem upward toward the back also, and attach with stitches. Clip off excess stem.

8 The base of flower becomes the top of the foxglove floret. Attach to a stem in a staggered or alternate arrangement. Continue making "quarter" roses until your foxglove is the desired height.

Completed foxglove.

Block Twelve:

Winter Window

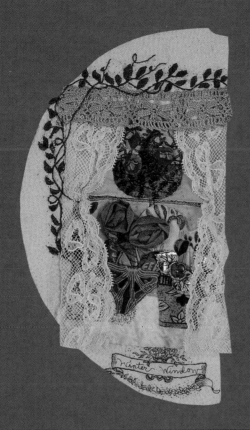

Featured Flowers:

Poppies,

Instructions

p. 139

Appliquéd Pansies,

Instructions

p. 143

The Winter of Celia's Life

""When the snow is still blowing against the window-pane in January and February, and the wild winds are howling without, what pleasure it is to plan for the summer that is to be!" [1]

Celia Thaxter
An Island Garden

The winter of 1877 was the last winter Celia was to spend on the island. She would no longer have to experience the harsh weather conditions and isolation that she had endured for so many years. With both parents now gone, Celia's responsibilities to others were lessening.

Now she spent most of her winters in Portsmouth, New Hampshire, the city of her birth, though she would continue to spend her summers in her cottage on Appledore. Waiting for winter to pass, Celia would paint china, which provided her with sufficient income to keep her comfortable during her last years. Her love of flowers was not seasonal; she continued to grow them throughout the winter, as her mother had so long ago in the lighthouse.

Celia's winter quarters in Portsmouth were very comfortable, with nine rooms and lots of sunny windows. There was plenty of room for Karl and his workshop, a room for Minna, her companion, and one for Oscar. Celia kept the windows full of blooming flowers and would look forward to tending them each day. She also tended to herself, "I am a great deal better, and getting well fast under a treatment I discovered and apply myself. No doctors, thank you." [2]

From the time Levi died in 1884, Celia had begun to experience again the freedom she had once known. Every day was precious and beautiful as it had been in her youth. However, the many years of anxiety and

hard work had taken their toll physically. During her last years she suffered from attacks of angina that left her quite helpless.

Celia writes of her agonies in an 1889 letter to John Greenleaf Whittier: "You cannot know what a joy your dear letter is to me...Yes, I had a quiet, lovely winter in Portsmouth. I did more writing than for years, and was well and content until about three weeks ago, when I was suddenly very ill...I do not mind the thought of death, it means only a fuller life, but there is a pang in the thought of leaving Karl...." [3]

But Celia continued to dream of summers to come and being out on her island home. To see the sparkling ocean in all its moods, to watch the sun break through so gloriously into a new day, and to watch it gently close the day were all part of Celia's being. She would begin to prepare for her summer garden in the dead of winter. "When the snow is still blowing against the windowpane in January and February, and the wild winds are howling without, what pleasure it is to plan for the summer that is to be!" [4]

As spring approached Celia would begin to grow seedlings for her summer garden. She would grow the delicate seeds of her poppies, which required special care, using the shells of eggs as planting containers. She would take everything with her when she went to the island in the spring.

Year after year, visitors came out to Appledore to see Celia's garden and marvel at her beautiful flowers.

They would try to garden as she did in their own plots on the mainland, but to no avail. They would return to Celia and ask the secrets of her beautiful garden. Celia was urged to write a book about it.

Sarah Orne Jewett, one of Celia's dearest friends and an author herself, offered to give Celia the help she needed to write a garden book. She encouraged Celia during the bleakest moments of her last winter. With Sarah's encouragement and help, *An Island Garden* was completed and published in 1894.

Much more than a how-to-garden manual, the book tells of Celia's love affair with her island garden and the flowers she lovingly planted each year. She describes the personality and beauty of each flower, and also describes the seasonal changes that take place in a garden.

Childe Hassam, America's foremost impressionist painter in the late nineteenth century, vacationed on Appledore and was fascinated by Celia's garden and parlor. He painted these special places hundreds of

Right: Celia holding her first grandson Charles Eliot, 1888. Photo courtesy of the University of New Hampshire, Dimond Library, Isles of Shoals Collection.

times, and some of his finest works were included in *An Island Garden*.

Flowers were not the only thing that gave Celia pleasure in the winter of her life. Her first grandchildren, her son Roland's children, were the loves of her life. Her son John's only child, Rosamond, was born a few months after Celia's death in 1894. Although Rosamond was never held in her grandmother's arms, she was devoted to Celia all her life and wrote her biography *Sandpiper*.

Celia's three children had been born while she herself was still a child. She had not been able to truly enjoy them as children. However, she was given a second chance with her grandchildren and they delighted her to no end. As Celia's winter was drawing to a close, she enjoyed these grandchildren given to her and savored every moment that remained.

My Winter Window quilt block represents Celia's last winters spent in Portsmouth, New Hampshire, in a home with blooming plants in each window. As I read a letter she had sent to a friend describing the riot of colorful blooms, I could visualize this window and its myriad of blooms.

I designed the half block to represent this winter garden and added antique lace for curtains, a bit of embroidery, flower buttons, and fabric flowers.

Instructions follow for the pansies and poppies that Celia grew as seedlings in her window for transplanting to her island garden.

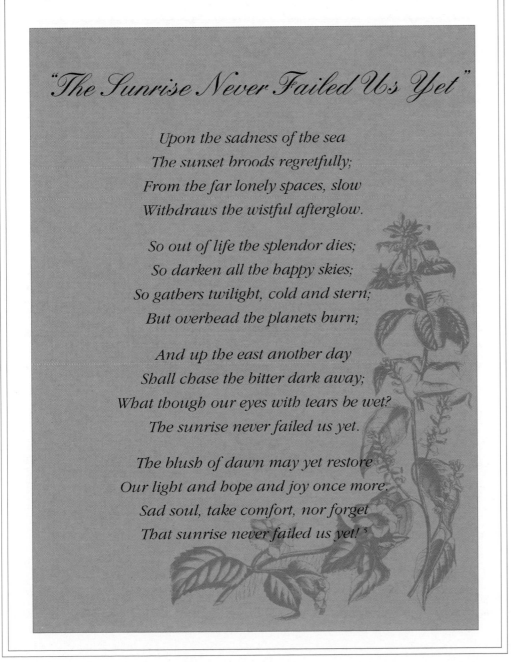

"*The Sunrise Never Failed Us Yet*"

Upon the sadness of the sea
The sunset broods regretfully;
From the far lonely spaces, slow
Withdraws the wistful afterglow.

So out of life the splendor dies;
So darken all the happy skies;
So gathers twilight, cold and stern;
But overhead the planets burn;

And up the east another day
Shall chase the bitter dark away;
What though our eyes with tears be wet?
The sunrise never failed us yet.

The blush of dawn may yet restore
Our light and hope and joy once more.
Sad soul, take comfort, nor forget
That sunrise never failed us yet! [5]

Winter Window

Winter Window Wreath from Elly Sienkiewicz *Baltimore Beauties and Beyond, Vol. II – Studies in Classic Album Quilt Appliqué*
Pattern 7, Volume II, C & T Publishing, page 118, Heart Medallion Frame.

POPPIES

Poppies symbolize forgetfulness, vanity, and fantastic extravagance.

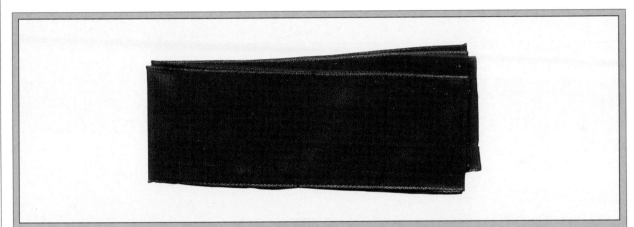

1 Use 36 inches of ½ inch wide wire-edged red-orange ribbon per flower.

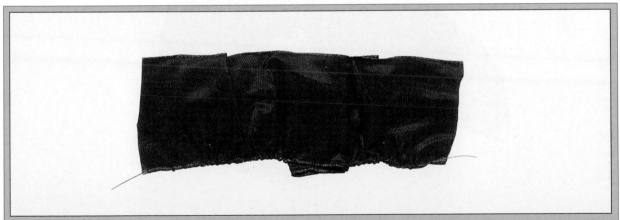

2 Expose about one inch of wire from both ends of one side of the ribbon. Gently bend wire back over the ribbon to keep it from sliding back. Work one end of the ribbon at a time. Hold the wire with your fingertips or use tweezers and gently slide the ribbon to the center of the ribbon's length with your other hand. Be gentle and slow. Do not force or rush the process. The wire might break, requiring a needle and thread to complete the gathering process. When the ribbon is half gathered fairly tightly (without forcing), turn to the opposite end and repeat the above process until all the ribbon is gathered.

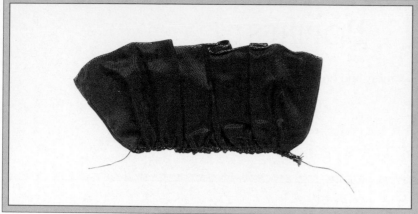

3 To keep the ribbon from ungathering, secure the finished portion by wrapping the wire around itself and the selvage edge. Do this on both ends of the gathered ribbon.

4 Form a flat circle with the gathered ribbon and pin together to hold the shape.

5 Continue to form the ribbon in a circular pattern around the center opening. You can gradually make the opening smaller with each layer, thereby giving the poppy a tapered and layered appearance. Stitch the inner selvage edges to each other to secure the flower layers.

6 Use black embroidery floss or drapery trim to form a center for the poppy. Insert this into the center opening. Attach the flower to the background fabric through the flower center.

Appliquéd Pansies

APPLIQUÉD PANSIES

P ansies symbolize, "you occupy my thoughts."

1 Trace the three pansy templates onto the paper or dull side of the freezer paper and cut out right on the line.

2 Iron the templates onto fabric, placing the shiny side onto the top or right side of the fabric and cut beyond the freezer paper a scant ¼". The freezer paper represents the sewing line.

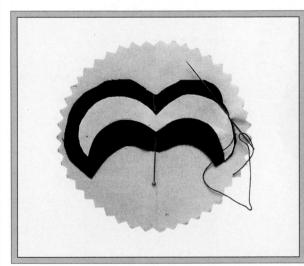

3 Using the tip of needle turn under the fabric to the edge of the freezer paper. Stitch in place using matching thread. An appliqué needle or milliners needle makes easy work of appliqué. Continue needleturning and stitching down the first crown petals of the pansy. Leave the freezer paper in place as a placement guide for the next petal.

4 Position the second petal onto the first petal. When you are pleased with its placement, pin in place and remove the freezer paper from the first petal. With matching thread, stitch the second petal in place.

5 Position the third or bottom petal into place and stitch. Use a marking pen or embroidery to add inked whiskers radiating out from the beaded flower center. Embroider the stem and appliqué leaves in place for a delightful appliquéd pansy.

6 Completed flower.

Block Thirteen:

Celia's Grave

A Poet's Burial

"When I saw Celia lying there the thought came to me that surely anyone so gifted and so beloved could not be lost forever." [1]

Oscar Laighton
Ninety Years on the Isles of Shoals

Featured Flower:

Rosebuds,

Instructions

p. 149

Celia's circle of life was almost complete. Perhaps she had a premonition of her mortality as she wrote this letter to ornithologist Bradford Torrey, little more than a month before her death: "I scribble this little line flying, as it were, to beg you, when the whirl of people passes and tranquility settles once more upon our little world, to steal a moment and slip down here and let us see and know you; will you not? Some of us may be slipping out of this mortal state, and we shall never know each other in this particular phase of existence, which would be a pity, I think." [2]

Celia's two dearest friends, Annie Fields and Sarah Orne Jewett, have recorded the passing of Celia with such poignant words, that it is only appropriate to end this tribute to Celia Thaxter with their reminiscences.

Sarah Orne Jewett relates: "Those who have known through her writings alone the islands she loved so much, may care to know how, just before she died, she paid, as if with dim foreboding, a last visit to the old familiar places of the tiny world that was so dear to her. Day after day she called those who were with her to walk or sail...Under the very rocks and gray ledges, to the far nests of the wild sea birds, her love and knowledge seemed to go. She was made of that very dust...but it seemed as if a little star dust must have mixed with the ordinary dust of those coasts; there was something bright in her spirit that will forever shine." [3]

Celia was feeling poorly on August 25, 1894. Her family was summoned from nearby Kittery Point, Maine to spend the next day with her. She seemed to rally with the presence of her sons and their families, spending a happy day with Roland beside her holding her hand, reading some of her poems and enjoying her grandchildren.

She seemed fine when she retired for the evening. Her beloved Minna was always close at hand and slept in the same room as Celia to see to her every need. As they were retiring, Celia asked Minna to raise the curtains so she could see the morning light. Celia so enjoyed seeing the glory of each new day unfold in a sunrise. Minna turned to Celia, after opening the curtains, and could see Celia was fading. In an instant Celia was gone. Celia had died on August 26, 1894, at age 59.

Her friend Annie Fields relates: "And so, indeed, Celia Thaxter slipped away from those who loved her, leaving suddenly this beautiful, sorrowful world, wherein she had loved and rejoiced and sorrowed with the children of men. No letters, no records, no description, can express adequately the richness and tenderness of her nature; but in a vanishing of her large vitality she has drawn many a heart after her to scan more closely than ever before the slight veil swaying between the seen and the unseen. [4]

She continues: "The burial was at her island, on a quiet afternoon in the late summer...It was indeed a poet's burial, but it was far more than that: it was the celebration of the passing of a large and beneficent soul...." [5]

And as the last words were spoken, a small bird was seen fluttering heavenward.

Though this block was one of the first to be designed, it was the last block to be stitched. There are three simple design elements – the hilltop where Celia was buried, a layer of fern-printed materials to represent the bed of sweet bay surrounding her coffin, and dimensional rosebuds covering her grave. I used fabric instead of ribbon to fashion a thick dimensional rosebud, layering those around the grave area to represent the huge mound of flowers that were heaped on Celia's grave.

Just as Celia tended her garden with her own two hands, you can create wonderful ribboned flowers. The wired ribbon will turn into beautiful blooms with a little care and attention.

Left: Celia's grave on the day of her burial August 28, 1894, Appledore. Photograph by Karl Thaxter. Photo courtesy of the University of New Hampshire, Dimond Library, Isles of Shoals Collection.

Celia's Grave Block

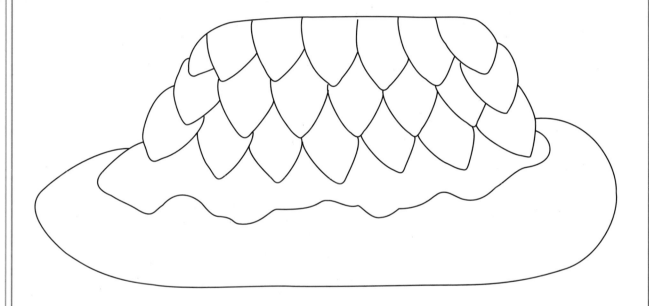

The Grave block is reduced 80% to fit the page. Enlarge by 125% to reproduce full-size.

ROSEBUDS

Pink rosebuds symbolize the lovely gentleness of a young girl.

1 Use a 3 inch square of fabric or ribbon per bud. Various widths of ribbon may be used. The proportion of length to width is 2-to-1.

Note: These rosebuds may also be made with unwired ribbon.

2 Fold fabric in half and press to mark the center fold. Fold the left half over toward the right section.

3 Fold the right side over the first fold. Leave an opening at the center top of about ⅛ inch.

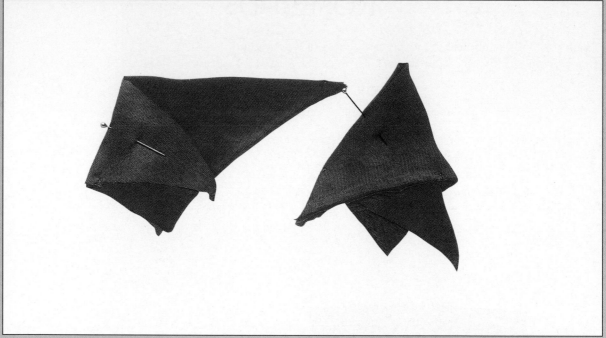

4 Pin to hold together. Trim uneven bottom edges into a semicircle.

5 Use a double thread and stitch a row of running stitches approximately ⅛ inch from the bottom edge.

6 Pull thread and "gather ye rosebuds." Secure thread and snip.

7 For a more complicated version of the above bud, fold the selvage edge over onto itself just before you stitch across the bottom edge.

Block Fourteen:

The Pansy Wreath

And many a maiden fairer yet,
Came smiling to my garden gate,
Some graceful head I decked alway
With pansy and with mignonette

from "My Garden"

The Garden Blooms Again

"...there was something bright in her spirit
that will forever shine,
and light the hearts of those who loved her." [1]
Sarah Orne Jewett

After Celia's burial beside her parents, family and friends returned to Celia's parlor. For over two hours they sat and listened to William Mason play music Celia had loved to hear. Her parlor was filled with her flowers, arranged by Appleton Brown and Childe and Maud Hassam, who knew how Celia would have wished everything organized.

Several friends of Celia's took responsibility for Karl, who stayed with them for some time and then eventually moved to Worcester, Massachusetts, where he lived until his death in 1912. Cedric and Oscar struggled to keep the Appledore House running smoothly, but many regular guests simply stopped coming. With Celia's passing, a major part of the charm of Appledore was gone forever. It was a difficult time financially for the Laighton brothers.

Cedric had married in 1881. He and his family moved into Celia's cottage where they continued to care for her garden and parlor. They did the best they could to keep it as Celia would have liked it, but they

Right: Celia's brother Cedric Laighton. Photo courtesy of the University of New Hampshire, Dimond Library, Isles of Shoals Collection.

Left: Celia's brother Oscar Laighton. Photo courtesy of the University of New Hampshire, Dimond Library, Isles of Shoals Collection.

were not blessed with her love and devotion.

When Cedric died suddenly in 1899, Oscar was devastated: "...we had always been together and depended upon each other. I was about ready to give up the ship, but struggled on, ever hoping for better seasons, and that I might be able to save something for Cedric's children, Ruth, Margaret, and Barbara, who were growing up fine girls and were a great comfort to me."[2]

Appledore and Star Island were purchased by the Star Island Corpora-

tion for their summer conferences, and this saved the islands. Oscar remained welcome on Star Island where he had a home until he died at the of ninety-nine years and nine months.

One day in September 1914, after the Appledore Hotel had closed for the season, there was a fire that began with a workman's spark, and the 60-year old hotel quickly went up in flames. Winds spread the fire to nearby cottages. Seeing the fire from Star Island, Oscar barely had time to get to his sister's cottage and rescue a few of her possessions

before it, too, was engulfed in flames. The smoke was visible from the mainland and drew large crowds along the shore. Memories of the grand hotel were all that remained after the flames died down.

Oscar was now alone with only his memories of the family and hotel that had been his life. He would spend his remaining years on Star Island, taking conference guests around the islands in his little boat, "Twilight." His tour narrative of how it had once been and of his beloved sister and her garden were remembered by many who attended conferences there.

Appledore was abandoned after the fire, and Celia's garden became overrun by island vegetation. Brambles and poison ivy choked her garden. It remained this way until the 1970's when the University of New Hampshire and Cornell University leased Appledore Island for the Shoals Marine Laboratory. In 1977, Dr. John Kingsbury, Director of the Shoals Marine Lab, discovered the remains of Celia's cottage while surveying the island. Using the garden posts found in front of the cottage and Celia's garden plan as presented in her *Island Garden* book, his group with much effort were able to resurrect the garden.

Today, as head gardener, Virginia Chislom lovingly tends Celia's plants. Sprouted by the University of New Hampshire, plants are transported out to the island each spring on the "Thomas B. Laighton" by Captain Robert Whittaker. Visitors can visit Celia's garden and enjoy her flowers today, as she did over 100 years ago.

Celia Thaxter has inspired many

Right: The garden blooms again. Celia's restored garden on Appledore. Photo: Faye Labanaris.

Left: Back of the quilt, *A TRIBUTE TO CELIA THAXTER.* A French pima cotton, purchased in NYC, was used to back the quilt. The fabric's print is filled with images of Celia's parlor. Photo: Richard Walker.

people. Donna Marion Titus, an artist, dramatic interpreter of Celia's life, and friend of Celia's today had this to say about Celia and my quilt: "'A Tribute to Celia Thaxter'... is appropriate to the poet who lived on Appledore at the Isles of Shoals over one hundred years ago. Roses, poppies, hollyhocks, and other old-fashioned garden flowers climb along the borders, and each square within has a special meaning."

She continues, "I have come to the conclusion that Celia is a touchstone to what is primitive within us. Perhaps that's a strange thing to say about a Victorian lady poet! But it is the contradictions of Thaxter, and there are many, that are the most fascinating...here we are, one hundred years later, still telling her story, still keeping her alive in words, pictures, flowers... and quilts."

Larkspur and Hummingbird

LARKSPUR AND HUMMINGBIRD

LARKSPUR

1 The larkspur blossoms are composed of several dozen individual lily-of-the-valley (instructions page 31) blooms clustered together along a green stem. The flowerettes were cut form a dyed purple fabric to give a shaded or variegated look to the blooms. Embroider the stems with a dark green thread.

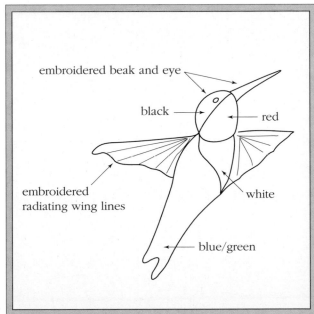

embroidered beak and eye

black

red

embroidered radiating wing lines

white

blue/green

HUMMINGBIRD

1 Cut a 2" square piece each of black and red fabric. Stitch together and press the seam to the black side. Trace the head unit onto a piece of clear template plastic. Be sure to include the diagonal line.

2 Cut out the head unit template and place onto the black-red fabric. Position the diagonal line to lie on the seam line. Trace the outline of the template onto the fabric with a marking pencil. This line represents your appliqué sewing line. Cut ¼" beyond the drawn line. You may leave a wider cutting margin at the neck edge for sewing ease.

3 Make a template for the entire body, including the chest area, label and cut apart. Trace the body template onto a piece of blue-green fabric, such as a large scale tropical print. Cut ¼" beyond the sewing line.

4 Stitch the upper body – chest edge to a piece of white fabric. Press the seam to the dark fabric side. Position the chest template and trace the neck and outer edge of the body. Stitch the head unit to the body unit.

5 Trace and cut the wings from dark blue fabric. Place under the hummingbird's body, positioning them so that the wing top edge meets the neck seam.

6 Stitch the entire bird into place. Embroidered details for the beak, eye, and radiating wing lines complete the appliqué.

Pansy Wreath

PANSIES

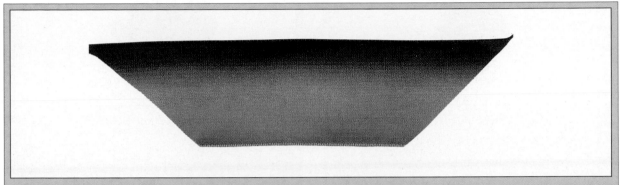

1 Cut one 6 inch strip of ½ inch wide wire-edged ombré ribbon per flower. Cut the end sections off at a 45 degree angle as indicated in diagram.

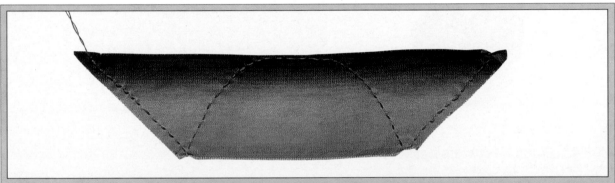

2 Use a 36 inch length of thread, matching one of the colors in the ribbon. Double the thread and knot the end. Stitch a row of tiny running stitches approximately ⅛ inch inside the cut edge. Continue stitching in the shape of a wide rounded petal in the center section. Finish stitching up the end cut edge. Leave needle and thread attached.

3 Gently pull the thread and gather the ribbon tightly.

Reprinted by the permission of C & T Publishing. Originally published in Elly Sienkiewicz's
Dimensional Appliqué: Baskets, Blooms & Baltimore Borders.

4 Secure the thread with a couple of overlapping stitches and cut the thread.

5 Fold the single bottom petal up over itself until it meets the two top petals.
Note: This is now the back of the flower.

6 Turn the flower over and adjust the lower petal "apron" until it meets the two top petals. The sides should touch. Top petals will have to be molded or sculpted to a round shape. Secure the top petals to the side of the lower petal with a few hidden stitches using a single matching thread.

7 Flower center may be heavily beaded at this point, or you can wait to bead when you attach the flower to the background fabric.

Note: Flower colors may be reversed by cutting the ribbon edges (Step 1) in the opposite manner, thus giving you two different flowers from the same piece of ombré ribbon.

NASTURTIUMS

Nasturtiums symbolize patriotism.

1 Cut 5 inches of 1½ inch wide wire-edged red-orange ribbon per flower.

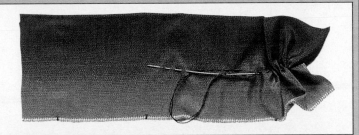

2 Select a matching thread and cut a piece approximately 36 inches in length, doubled and knotted. Stitch a row of running stitches through the middle of the ribbon lengthwise, starting and stopping in ⅛" from the cut edges.

3 Gather tightly and end with 2 or 3 overlapping stitches.

4 Fold gathered ribbon in half lengthwise, and seam the cut edges together with a narrow seam.
Note: The top edge will be both selvage edges, and the bottom edge will be the stitched and gathered section.

5 Trace a leaf template from the leaf given. *Note:* This is the cutting line. Add a seam allowance of ⅛ to 3/16" for needle turning.

6 Unfold gathered ribbon nasturtium and press flat with fingers. Beads may be stitched in the center of the flower at this point, or you can wait until the flower is in place on the background fabric. The beads and anchoring stitches can be done simultaneously.

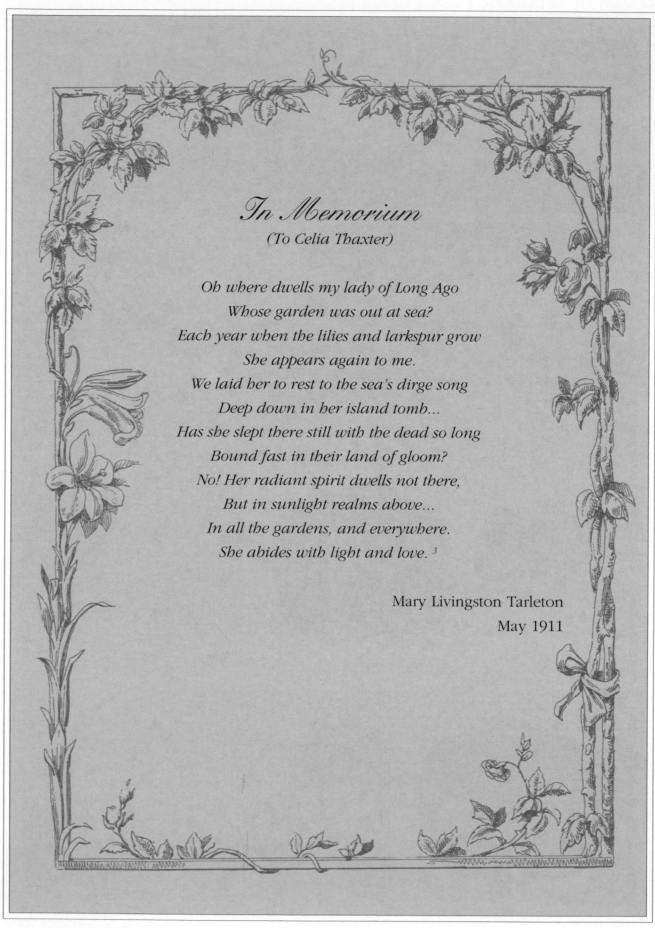

In Memorium
(To Celia Thaxter)

Oh where dwells my lady of Long Ago
Whose garden was out at sea?
Each year when the lilies and larkspur grow
She appears again to me.
We laid her to rest to the sea's dirge song
Deep down in her island tomb...
Has she slept there still with the dead so long
Bound fast in their land of gloom?
No! Her radiant spirit dwells not there,
But in sunlight realms above...
In all the gardens, and everywhere.
She abides with light and love. [3]

Mary Livingston Tarleton
May 1911

Endnotes

INTRODUCTION; PAGES 1–16

1. Oscar Laighton, *Ninety Years at the Isles of Shoals.* (Boston, MA: The Beacon Press, Inc., 1930), p. 139.

BLOCK ONE: CELIA'S PROFILE – CELIA THAXTER: POET, GARDENER, LOVER OF NATURE; PAGES 17–26

1. Roseamond Thaxter, *Sandpiper The Life & Letters of Celia Thaxter* (Francestown, NH: Marshall Jones Company; 1963), p. 6.

2. Maud Appleton Brown, "Childhood Memories" in *Heavenly Guest with Other Unpublished Writings by Celia Thaxter,* edited by Oscar Laighton, (Andover, Mass: Smith & Coutts Co. Printers, 1935), p. 127.

3. Letter to John, 1880 from Vaughn Cottage/Thaxter Museum. Transcribed by Fred McGill and Donna Titus.

4. Letter dated Feb. 25, 1861 from Celia to Mother.

5. Celia Thaxter, *The Poems of Celia Thaxter* Appledore edition by Roland Thaxter (Boston & New York: Houghton, Mifflin and Company, 1899), p. 162.

6. Ibid., p. 209.

7. *Letters of Celia Thaxter,* edited by her Friends A. F. and R. L. (Boston & New York: Houghton, Mifflin and Co., 1895), note.

6. Thaxter, *The Poems of Celia Thaxter,* p. 162.

BLOCK TWO: ISLES OF SHOALS MAP – THE ENCHANTED ISLES; PAGES 27–32

1. Celia Thaxter, *Among the Isles of Shoals* (Boston: James R. Osgood & Co., 1873), p. 7.

2. Ibid., p. 9–11.

3. Ibid., p. 14.

4 Ibid., p. 7–8.

BLOCK THREE: THE FAMILY TREE – THE LAIGHTON-THAXTER LEGEND BEGINS; PAGES 33–40

1. Oscar Laighton, *Ninety Years at the Isles of Shoals* (Boston: The Beacon Press, Inc., 1930), p. 6–7.

2. Thaxter, *Among the Isles of Shoals*, p. 120.

3. Laighton, p. 2.

BLOCK FOUR: THE LIGHTHOUSE YEARS; PAGES 41–48

1. Thaxter, *Among the Isles of Shoals*, p. 120.

2 . Ibid., p. 121.

3. Lyman V. Rutledge, *The Isles of Shoals in Lore and Legend* (Boston, MA: The Star Island Corporation, 1971), p. 64–65.

4. Laighton, p. 15.

5. Ibid., p. 14–15.

6. Thaxter, *Among the Isles of Shoals*, p. 133.

7. Letter to Whittier, April 11, 1889. *Letters of Celia Thaxter,* p. 133.

8. Thaxter, *Among the Isles of Shoals*, p. 133.

BLOCK FIVE: SANDPIPER BLOCK – CAREFREE DAYS OF YOUTH; PAGES 49–56

1. Thaxter, *Among the Isles of Shoals*, p. 123.

2. Ibid., p. 124.

3. Ibid., p. 128.

4. Ibid., p. 129.

5. Ibid., p. 133.

6. Ibid., p. 131–132.

7. Laighton, p. 16.

8. Thaxter, *The Poems of Celia Thaxter*, p. 18.

BLOCK SIX: THE PINAFORE – LEVI THAXTER; PAGES 57–66

1. Thaxter, *The Poems of Celia Thaxter*, p. 25.

2. Laighton, p. 15.

3. Ibid, p. 15.

4. Rutledge, p. 78.

5. Laighton, p. 45.

6. Thaxter, *The Poems of Celia Thaxter*, p. 195.

BLOCK SEVEN: THE APPLEDORE HOUSE; PAGES 67–80

1. Laighton, p. 101.

2. Roseamond Thaxter, *Sandpiper The Life & Letters of Celia Thaxter* (Francestown, NH: Marshall
    Jones Company; 1963), p. 26.

3. Laighton, p. 101.

4. Maria Parloa, *The Appledore Cookbook Containing Practical Recipes for Plain and Rich Cooking*
    (Boston: Andrew F. Graves, 1880), p. 4.

5. Ibid, p. 147.

6. Ibid, p. 97.

7. Ibid, p. 210.

8. Ibid, p. 18.

BLOCK EIGHT: A DAWN OF CHANGE; PAGES 81–90

1. Laighton, p. 48.

2. Ibid, p. 48.

3. Rutledge, p. 80.

4. Rosamond, Thaxter, p. 62.

5. Thaxter, *The Poems of Celia Thaxter*, p. 1.

BLOCK NINE: YEARS OF CONFLICT: DAUGHTER, MOTHER, WIFE AUTHOR; PAGES 91–102

1. Thaxter, *Letters of Celia Thaxter*, p. 24.

2. Ibid., p. 4–5.

3. Jane E. Vallier, *Poet on Demand – The Life, Letters and Works of Celia Thaxter*, 2nd Edition
    (Portsmouth, NH: Peter E. Randall Publisher, 1982, 1994), p. 96.

4. Ibid., p. 96.

5. Rosamond Thaxter, p. 121.

BLOCK TEN: CELIA'S PARLOR; PAGES 103–114

I. Celia Thaxter, *An Island Garden*, (Boston, MA: Houghton, Mifflin & Co., 1894), p.102.

2. Rutledge, p. 129.

3. Colby Quarterly, p. 521.

4. Thaxter, *An Island Garden*, p. 103.

5. Ibid, p. 93–94.

6. Celia Thaxter, *The Heavenly Guest with Other Unpublished Writings*, edited by Oscar Laighton,
    (Andover, MA: Smith & Coutts Co., 1935), p. 126.

7. Ibid, p. 121–122.

8. Thaxter, *An Island Garden*, p. 99.

9. *Letters of Celia Thaxter*, Preface pages XXVIII–XXIX.

10. Thaxter, *An Island Garden*, p. 99.

BLOCK ELEVEN: CELIA'S GARDEN; PAGES 115–132

1. Thaxter, *Heavenly Guest*, p. 91.

2. Thaxter, *An Island Garden*, p. 113.

3. Ibid. p. 5.

4. Candace Wheeler, *Content in a Garden*, (Boston, MA: Houghton, Mifflin & Co., 1901), p. 118.

5. Thaxter, *An Island Garden*, p. 9.

6. Ibid, p. 112.

7. Ibid, p. 111.

8. Thaxter, *Poems of Celia Thaxter*, p. 205.

BLOCK TWELVE: THE WINTER OF CELIA'S LIFE; PAGES 133–144

1. Thaxter, *An Island Garden*, p. 15.

2. *Letters of Celia Thaxter*, p. 157.

3. Ibid, p. 159.

4. Thaxter, *An Island Garden*, p. 15.

5. Thaxter, *Poems of Celia Thaxter*, p. 142.

BLOCK THIRTEEN: CELIA'S DEATH; PAGES 145–150

1. Laughton, p. 139.

2. Thaxter, *Letters of Celia Thaxter*, p. 219.

3. *Poems of Celia Thaxter*, p. VI – VIII.

4. *Letters of Celia Thaxter*, p. 220.

5. Ibid, p. 222.

BLOCK FOURTEEN: THE GARDEN TODAY; PAGES 151–160

1. Thaxter, *Poems of Celia Thaxter*, p. VIII.

2. Laighton, p. 145.

3. In Memorium poem, from Vaughn Cottage Archive #MS 547.44. Star Island Corporation.

Bibliography

Bardwell, John D. *The Isles of Shoals A Visual History*. Portsmouth, NH: Peter E. Randall Publisher, 1989.

Curry, David Park. *Childe Hassam An Island Garden Revisited*. New York: Denver Art Museum in association with W. W Norton & Company, 1990.

Fields, Annie. *Authors and Friends*. Boston and New York: Houghton, Mifflin and Company, 1893, 1896.

Jenness, John Scribner. *The Isles of Shoals An Historical Sketch*. Boston: Houghton Mifflin and Company, 1884.

Laighton, Oscar. *Ninety Years at the Isles of Shoals*. Boston: The Beacon Press, Inc., 1930.

Letters of Celia Thaxter Edited by Her Friends. A.F. and R.L. Boston and New York: Houghton, Mifflin and Company, 1895.

Mason, Caleb. *The Isles of Shoals Remembered A Legacy from America's Musician and Artists' Colony*. Boston: Charles E. Tuttle Company, Inc. 1992.

Parloa, Maria. *The Appledore Cook Book Containing Practical Recipes of Plain and Rich Cooking*. Boston, MA: Andrew F. Graves, 1880.

Randall, Peter. *Out on the Shoals*. Portsmouth, NH: Peter E. Randall Publisher, 1995.

Roman, Judith A. *Annie Adams Fields - The Spirit of Charles Street*. Bloomington & Indianapolis: Indiana University Press, 1990.

Rutledge, Lyman V. *The Isles of Shoals in Lore and Legend*. Boston, MA: The Star Island Corporation, 1965.

Rutledge, Lyman V. *Ten Miles Out Guide Book to the Isles of Shoals, Portsmouth, N.H.* Boston, MA: Isles of Shoals Association, 1984.

A Stern and Lovely Scene: A Visual History of the Isles of Shoals. Durham, NH: University Art Galleries, University of New Hampshire, 1978.

Sterns, Frank Preston. *Sketches From Concord and Appledore*. New York: G. P. Putnam's Sons, 1895.

Thaxter, Celia. *Among the Isles of Shoals*. Boston: James R. Osgood & Co, 1873. Reissued. Portsmouth, NH: Peter Randall E. Randall Publisher, 1994.

Thaxter, Celia. *The Heavenly Guest with Other Unpublished Writings*. Edited by Oscar Laighton. Andover, MA: Smith & Coutts Co. Printers, 1935.

Thaxter, Celia. *An Island Garden*. Boston: Houghton, Mifflin and Company, 1894, 1988.

Thaxter, Celia. *The Poems of Celia Thaxter*. Boston: Houghton, Mifflin and Company, 1896, 1899. Portsmouth, NH: Peter E. Randall Publisher, 1996.

Thaxter, Celia. *Stories and Poems for Children.* Boston: Houghton, Mifflin and Company, 1895.

Thaxter, Rosamond. *Sandpiper – The Life and Letters of Celia Thaxter and Her Home on the Isles of Shoals – Her Family, Friends & Favorite Poems.* Francestown, NH: Marshall Jones Company, 1963.

Vallier, Jane E. *Poet on Demand – The Life, Letters and Works of Celia Thaxter.* Portsmouth, NH: Peter E. Randall Publisher, 1982, 1994.

Wheeler, Candance. *Content in a Garden.* Boston, MA: Houghton, Mifflin & Co., 1901.

Whittaker, Robert H. *Land of Lost Content: The Piscatagua River Basin and the Isles of Shoals. The People. Their Dream. Their History.* Alan Sutton Publishing Inc., Dover, NH 1993.

Resources

For information send a long SASE.

WIRE-EDGED RIBBON

Wholesale only from:
Quilters' Resource, Inc.
P.O. Box 148850
Chicago, IL 60614
800 676-6543

Wire-edged Ribbon Kit to make Celia's Flowers
Faye Labanaris
80 Mt. Vernon Street
Dover, NH 03820-2726
603 742-0211

BOOKS

Related to Celia Thaxter and the Isles of Shoals
Peter E. Randall, Publisher
P.O. Box 4726
Portsmouth, NH 03802
603 431-5667
Send a long SASE with 55 cent postage for a list of books available.

FABRIC

Hand-painted fabric from Mickey Lawler
Skydyes
83 Richmand Lane
West Hartford, CT 06117
203 232-1429

Dyed fabric from Stacy Mitchell
Shades, Inc.
585 Cobb Parkway South
Nunn Complex, Studio O
Marietta, GA 30062-8202
800 783-3933

TRAVEL INFORMATION

To visit Celia's garden on Appledore Island, contact:
Shoals Marine Laboratory
G-14, Cornell University
Ithaca, NY 14853
607 254-2900

To visit Star Island, Isles of Shoals, contact:
Isles of Shoals Steamship Company
315 Market Street
Portsmouth, NH 03802
800 441-4620

WORKSHOPS

Faye Labanaris
80 Mt. Vernon Street
Dover, NH 03820-2726
603 742-0211

AQS Books on Quilts

This is only a partial listing of the books on quilts that are available from the American Quilter's Society. AQS books are known the world over for their timely topics, clear writing, beautiful color photographs, and accurate illustrations and patterns. Most of the following books are available from your local bookseller, quilt shop, or public library. If you are unable to locate certain titles in your area, you may order by mail from the AMERICAN QUILTER'S SOCIETY, P.O. Box 3290, Paducah, KY 42002-3290. Customers with Visa or MasterCard may phone in orders from 7:00–4:00 CST, Monday–Friday, Toll Free 1-800-626-5420. Add $2.00 for postage for the first book ordered and $0.40 for each additional book. Include item number, title, and price when ordering. Allow 14 to 21 days for delivery.